THE BRONTË SISTERS

THE BRONTË SISTERS

The Brief Lives of
CHARLOTTE, EMILY, AND ANNE

Catherine Reef

Houghton Mifflin Harcourt
Boston · New York

For information about permission to reproduce selections from this book,
write to Permissions, Houghton Mifflin Harcourt Publishing Company,
215 Park Avenue South, New York, New York 10003.

www.hmhco.com

The text of this book is set in Figural.

The Library of Congress has cataloged the hardcover edition as follows:
Reef, Catherine.
The Brontë sisters : the brief lives of Charlotte, Emily, and Anne / by Catherine Reef.
p. cm.
Includes bibliographical references.
1. Brontë, Charlotte, 1816–1855—Juvenile literature. 2. Brontë, Emily, 1818–1848—Juvenile
literature. 3. Brontë, Anne, 1820–1849—Juvenile literature. 4. Authors, English—19th
century—Biography—Juvenile literature. 5. Sisters—England—Yorkshire—Biography—
Juvenile literature. 6. Women authors, English—Biography—Juvenile literature. I. Title.
PR4168.R37 2012
823'.809—dc23 [B]   2011043559

ISBN: 978-0-547-57966-5 hardcover
ISBN: 978-0-544-45590-0 paperback

Printed in China
SCP 10 9 8 7 6 5 4 3 2 1
4500523833

For Karen Leggett,

a friend to children's literature

Contents

one

"Oh God, My Poor Children!"

THE cobbled road clung to the steep hill as if holding on for dear life. Its paving stones had been set on end, forming a series of little ledges. The nervous horses felt for these rocky shelves to gain a footing; they feared slipping down as they hauled their heavy load.

It was April 1820, and a new clergyman was coming to Haworth. The Reverend Patrick Brontë surveyed the scene. He told his wife and children that they were all strangers in a strange land.

Life was easy for no one in Haworth — not for horses, and not for people. Haworth, in northern England, was a dirty village of weavers' cottages, where death came early.

The soured earth barely fed some stunted bushes that struggled to stay alive. Few trees grew in this bleak place, where a sad wind constantly blew.

Beyond Haworth stretched miles and miles of moorland, that bare, hilly country of rough grass, moss, and bracken. The Brontë children would learn to love this strange, wild land.

There were six children when the family moved into the parsonage at the top of the hill. Six-year-old Maria helped care for the younger ones, because their mother was ailing. Mrs. Brontë had yet to recover from the birth of baby Anne, four months earlier, on January 17. The second child, Elizabeth, was five, and Charlotte, born on April 21,

Haworth Church overlooks the village from its hilltop. The tower still stands, but a later clergyman had the rest of the church torn down and rebuilt between 1879 and 1881.

1816, was turning four. Patrick Branwell (called Branwell) was not yet three, and Emily Jane, born on July 30, 1818, would be two in summer.

The children played quietly in an upstairs room while their mother, Maria Branwell Brontë, wasted away. The nature of her ailment remains unclear. She might have had cancer, or she might have acquired a lingering infection after Anne's birth. Antibiotics belonged to the future, so infections in the 1800s were often deadly. Her unmarried sister, Elizabeth Branwell, journeyed to Haworth from Cornwall, in the southwest, to nurse the sick woman.

The children turned to "Aunt" if they needed attention or care. They knew better than to bother their father in his study, where he wrote sermons and poems that taught moral lessons. In one poem, he revealed the dreary thoughts that ran through his head on a winter night.

> *Where Sin abounds Religion dies,*
> *And Virtue seeks her native skies;*
> *Chaste Conscience, hides for very shame,*
> *And Honour's but an empty name.*
> *Then, like a flood, with fearful din,*
> *A gloomy host, comes pouring in.*

This tall, redheaded clergyman was born Patrick Brunty in what is now Northern Ireland. His father was a farm laborer who could barely read, but Patrick wanted more from life. So he read books, taught school at sixteen, and caught the notice of an influential minister. This man saw that with an education, Patrick might become a fine clergyman, so he sent him to college in Cambridge, England. It was rare for an Irishman, especially one with such humble roots, to attend college in nineteenth-century Britain, but Patrick was uncommonly bright and ambitious. He distanced himself from his home and family even more when he changed his surname to Brontë, which sounded like the Greek word for thunder. He earned a degree in theology and was ordained a minister in 1806. He married Maria Branwell from Cornwall in 1812 and made England his home, returning to Ireland just once.

On September 15, 1821, Maria Branwell Brontë uttered her dying words: "Oh God, my poor children!" She became the first Brontë laid to rest under the stone slabs of Haworth's church. "I was left quite alone," her grieving husband wrote, "unless you suppose my six little children and the nurse and servants to have been company." His words implied that he did not. Hoping to marry again, he proposed to three women, one after another, but they all turned him down. None wanted a husband with a small income and a large family. Patrick Brontë remained single, and Elizabeth Branwell stayed on to oversee her late sister's household.

Somber Aunt Branwell dressed in black. Like other country women, Aunt Branwell walked in pattens, or platforms of wood or metal strapped to her shoes. Most women wore their pattens outdoors, to raise their skirts above the mud and dirt, but Aunt wore hers in the house to keep her feet off the cold stone floors. There were few carpets in the parsonage, and no curtains hung on the windows, because the Reverend Brontë had a great fear of fire. He kept a pail of water on the staircase landing to be ready to douse a flame in a moment.

Aunt Branwell taught the girls to sew while the Reverend Brontë took charge of Branwell's education. The clergyman had high hopes for his only son. He schooled Branwell in Latin and classical Greek, the subjects that formed the basis of a boy's education. Branwell and his sisters read three daily newspapers and their father's copies of *Blackwood's Magazine*. *Blackwood's* printed tales of country life, adventure, and ghosts. Charlotte was thrilled to read stories about Arthur Wellesley, the first Duke of Wellington. This great military leader had led the English forces in the 1815 Battle of Waterloo, in Belgium. England and its allies defeated Napoleon in this historic confrontation, ending decades of armed conflict between the English and French.

The children escaped from the parsonage whenever they could to ramble on the moor. In winter they clambered over hills of snow, and in warmer months they ran through banks of brown and purple heather. They learned the calls of grouse, swallows, and golden plovers, and at a favorite spot they plunged their hands into a cold, clear stream to fish for tadpoles. Anne and Emily named this place "The Meeting of the Waters," after a lyric that Anne loved by Thomas Moore, an Irish poet and songwriter.

Childhood felt as vast as the moor, but the youngsters' father saw its boundary. Patrick Brontë looked ahead to a time when his daughters might need to make their way in the world. Women with money enjoyed an advantage in the marriage market, and the Brontë girls had none. Like other fathers of his time, Patrick hoped to see his daughters marry, but he wanted to equip them for life in case they stayed single. The only profession open to respectable single women was teaching, so in July 1824, he sent the two oldest girls, Maria and Elizabeth, to the Clergy Daughters' School at Cowan Bridge, northwest of Haworth, to be suitably prepared. Charlotte joined them in August, and Emily followed in November. Someone wrote in the school's register book that Charlotte, age eight, was "altogether clever of her age." Emily, at six, "read prettily." But at Cowan Bridge, the Brontë girls soon learned lessons that were far different from the ones they expected.

Founded as a charity institution for the daughters of poor ministers, the school at Cowan Bridge was a place of suffering and abuse. The school's founder, the Reverend

Open, rolling hills and blustery skies: this is the Yorkshire moorland.

William Carus Wilson, saw sin wherever he looked, even in the faces of children. "Sin, like a full-blown weed, lies all before us, ready for the knife," he wrote. "In childhood, the seeds of inbred corruption spring up like luxuriant vegetation." Carus Wilson believed that the girls in his care would grow up to be sinners unless he intervened. As women, they would tempt men to do evil unless he set them on the right path. He employed cruel methods to teach Christian humility and stifle the students' emerging sexuality. The girls' hair symbolized beauty, so the school's staff cut it short. They kept the damp building cold in winter and fed the pupils small meals of burned porridge, stale bread, and rancid meat that turned even the emptiest stomach.

Any girl who was untidy had to wear a badge of public shame. This proved to be a big problem for Maria Brontë, who never could keep her nails clean or wash her face properly in the few drops of icy water she was given. Because of this shortcoming, a sadistic schoolmistress named Miss Andrews singled her out for punishment. Charlotte never forgot the day when Miss Andrews sent Maria to fetch a bundle of sticks. As Charlotte and the other girls looked on, she ordered the child to loosen the pinafore that covered her thin body. She then whipped Maria fiercely across the back of the neck with one of the sticks.

The Reverend William Carus Wilson founded the school at Cowan Bridge in January 1824, and Maria and Elizabeth Brontë came as pupils six months later. Carus Wilson meted out discipline that was strict to the point of cruelty.

It soon became clear that Maria was sick, but at Cowan Bridge, illness was no reason for pampering the body. One morning, Miss Andrews yanked the suffering girl from her bed, flung her to the middle of the dormitory, and scolded her for being dirty. Moving slowly and weakly, Maria got dressed, only to have Miss Andrews punish her for tardiness.

Her sister's mistreatment made Charlotte furious, but she had no power to stop it. Maria, however, believed it was her Christian duty to submit. "God waits only the separation of spirit from flesh to crown us with a full reward," she told Charlotte. "Why, then, should we ever sink overwhelmed with distress, when life is so soon over, and death is so certain an entrance to happiness?"

Before long, she passed through that entrance. In February 1825, the school's managers sent Maria home with an advanced case of the "graveyard cough": tuberculosis. This fearsome disease usually attacked the lungs, but it could spread to other organs as well. It was passed along when an infected person sneezed or coughed and sent tiny droplets into the air for someone else to inhale. People who contracted tuberculosis wasted away and died. They coughed up blood and soaked their bedding in perspiration. They ran a fever and exhausted themselves gasping for breath. They lost so much weight that the illness seemed to be eating up their bodies. This is why tuberculosis had another name: consumption. It was a relentless disease that would be blamed for a third of all deaths among English laborers in the 1830s.

All her siblings grieved when the eleven-year-old died in May, but Branwell and Charlotte felt the loss profoundly. Seven-year-old Branwell pored over lines in *Blackwood's Magazine* that mirrored his own sorrow:

> *Long, long, long ago, the time when we danced along, hand in hand with our golden-haired sister, whom all who looked on loved! — long, long, long ago, the day on which she died — the hour, so far more dismal than any hour that can now darken us on earth, when she — her coffin — and that velvet pall descended — and descended — slowly, slowly into the horrid clay, and we were borne deathlike, and wishing to die, out of the churchyard, that, from that moment, we thought we could enter never more!*

Branwell read this passage so many times that he could repeat it nearly word for word ten years later. As a teenager and young adult, Charlotte would tell her new friends about Maria's mistreatment, illness, and death.

Barely a month had passed since Maria's burial when a carriage pulled up to the Haworth parsonage. A servant

A building that housed the Clergy Daughters' School still stands beside a road in Lancashire, England.

from Cowan Bridge was bringing Elizabeth home because she, too, had advanced tuberculosis. Seeing Elizabeth's wasted condition, her frightened father removed Charlotte and Emily from the Clergy Daughters' School immediately, possibly saving their lives. The change came too late for Elizabeth, though. She died in June, at age ten. The family grieved, and Aunt Branwell drew close to little Anne.

The surviving girls continued their learning in the safety of home. Under their father's direction, they memorized passages from the Bible and studied grammar, geography, and history. The Reverend Brontë offered them classics from the past, like Shakespeare's plays and *Paradise Lost*,

John Milton's epic poem on the story of Adam and Eve. His shelves also held works by the Romantic poets of his own time, writers like William Wordsworth and George Gordon, Lord Byron. These poets let nature ignite their imaginations, and they valued feeling over logic and reasoning. When the Romantic poets spoke, the Brontë girls understood. Children who had known so much loss felt comforted thinking of nature as a steadfast friend.

"Nature never did betray / The heart that loved her," wrote Wordsworth, who lived in the scenic Lake District of northwest England:

> *tis her privilege,*
> *Through all the years of this our life, to lead*
> *From joy to joy. . . .*

The girls also enjoyed the verses of handsome Lord Byron, who died in 1824, having lived life to its fullest. He had traveled widely, had many love affairs, and fought in wars in Italy and Greece. In nature, he wrote, a person could "mingle with the Universe":

> *There is a pleasure in the pathless woods,*
> *There is rapture on the lonely shore,*
> *There is society where none intrudes,*
> *By the deep sea, and music in its roar.*

William Wordsworth stated famously that poetry is "emotion recollected in tranquility."

None of the children loved nature more than tall, quiet, independent Emily. On the moor, with a dog at her side, she found greater beauty and freedom than the others could see or feel. For Emily alone, "Flowers brighter than the rose bloomed in the blackest of the heath," Charlotte said. "She found in the bleak solitude many and dear delights." At home, Emily felt drawn to the kitchen, where she helped Tabby Aykroyd, the paid housekeeper, cook meals and bake bread.

Some of Lord Byron's poems told stories of moody, brooding young men, characters like the world-weary Childe Harold, who travels in foreign lands. Misunderstood, these figures live in exile from their homes, sometimes growing cynical and self-destructive. These Byronic heroes appealed to Branwell, who liked to imagine himself as a long-suffering outcast.

Diligent Charlotte was often reading, but she held books close to her face to aid her weak eyes. Charlotte was small for her age and had brown hair, like her sisters. A large forehead and a crooked mouth made her plain rather than pretty. Smart but not a showoff, Charlotte said "very little about herself" and was "averse from making any display of what she knew," her father noted. A passionate heart beat in Charlotte's chest, but she kept that hidden, too. She wanted to be a writer.

Tender Anne, the youngest, was Aunt Branwell's darling. She was petite like Charlotte and the only one with curls. She was a delicate child who suffered from asthma.

Lord Byron's colorful life and his wandering hero Childe Harold strongly influenced the Brontë children.

As an adult, Anne described herself in childhood, in a poem titled "Self-Communion":

> *I see, far back, a helpless child,*
> *Feeble and full of causeless fears,*
> *. . . . .*
> *More timid than the wild wood-dove*
> *Yet trusting to another's care,*
> *And finding in protecting love*
> *Its only refuge from despair.*

The four children were their own playmates, because their father had forbidden them to mix with the unwashed village youngsters. They liked to write and then read what one another had written. The girls wrote "diary papers" that were like snapshots of family life. In 1829, thirteen-year-old Charlotte put this scene on paper:

> *I am in the kitchen of the Parsonage, Haworth; Tabby, the servant, is washing up the breakfast things, and Anne, my youngest sister . . . is kneeling on a chair, look-ing at some cakes which Tabby has been baking for us. Emily is in the parlour, brushing the carpet. Papa and Branwell are gone to Keighley [the nearest large town]. Aunt is upstairs in her room, and I am sitting by the table writing this.*

Emily recorded people's actions as they were happening in one of her diary papers. She also captured a trace of Tabby's rustic accent:

Anne and I have been peeling apples for Charlotte to make an apple pudding. . . . Aunt has come into the kitchen just now and said where are your feet Anne[?] Anne answered On the floor Aunt[.] Papa opened the parlour door and gave Branwell a letter saying here Branwell read this and show it to your Aunt and Charlotte. . . . Tabby said on my putting a pen in her face Ya pitter pottering there instead of pilling [peeling] a potate[.] I answered O Dear, O Dear, O dear I will directly with that I get up, take a knife and begin pilling.

One night in June 1826, the Reverend Brontë returned from a trip to Leeds, bringing Branwell a set of toy soldiers. The next morning, Branwell took the soldiers to the bedroom that Charlotte and Emily shared. "I snatched one up and exclaimed, 'this is the Duke of Wellington! It shall be mine!'" Charlotte recalled years later. Emily chose one, too, and when Anne woke up, so did she. "Emily's was a grave-looking fellow. We called him Gravey," Charlotte said. "Anne's was a queer little thing very much like herself. He was called Waiting Boy. Branwell chose Bonaparte." (Branwell had read *The Life of the Emperor Napoleon*.) The children later renamed Gravey and Waiting Boy after two Arctic explorers, Sir William Parry and Captain John Ross.

This simple gift of wooden soldiers inspired a world of activity. The children invented intricate games, or "plays," to be acted by their soldier characters. In the first one, "Young Men," the soldiers conquered lands in Africa, that strange, far-off continent that the children read about in *Blackwood's Magazine*. The soldiers clashed with one another for power, but they eventually united to form the "Glass Town Confederacy." The four children were the "Genii," who could restore any soldier to life, to have him ready for the next game.

The games grew complex as the children created more characters to play out their fantasies: kings, dukes, explorers, and elegant women for the men to love and fight for. Charlotte and Branwell imagined a kingdom called Angria, where these figures acted their dramas. Emily and Anne got tired of the small roles assigned to them by their older siblings and withdrew to start their own saga. Their imaginary adventures happened in Gondal, an island nation in the Pacific. Gondal's ruler, King Julius, loved the beautiful but treacherous Augusta.

All four children knew how to draw, so they made maps of their territories and portraits of their favorite characters. They also wrote stories, poems, and imaginary histories of Angria and Gondal. In an action-packed story titled "The

Pirate," Branwell described a battle between one of his invented heroes, Alexander Percy, and Satan:

Crying, "I have done with thee, thou wretch", [Percy] took the ugly heap of mortality and hurled it into the sea. When it touched the water a bright flash of fire darted from it, changed it into a vast genius of immeasurable and indefinable height and size, and seizing hold of a huge cloud with his hand, he vaulted into it, crying: "And I've done with thee, thou fool" and disappeared among the passing vapours.

It is easy to imagine a boy acting out scenes like this with his toy figures, speaking their words aloud and adding sound effects.

Charlotte wrote on tiny pages in letters so minuscule that some could be read only with a magnifying glass. She then sewed these sheets into books. She often wrote from the characters' points of view, as if they were the real authors of the stories and poems she produced. She created historical accounts of Angria and its people, and she wrote out long scripts, imagining the poetic lines her characters would speak to each other.

Much of Branwell's and Charlotte's childhood writing has survived the passage of time, but most of Emily and Anne's early Gondal chronicles were either lost or

Such tiny books! Charlotte Brontë bound her childhood writings into volumes no taller than a woman's thumb.

destroyed. Emily copied forty-four of her Gondal poems into a notebook, but she was already eighteen years old when she wrote the first of these. (The Brontës continued to imagine life in Gondal and Angria even after they were grown.) Emily was a gifted poet, and the beauty and emotional power of her lines can affect even readers who have never heard of Gondal:

> *Come, the wind may never again*
> *Blow as now it blows for us*

And the stars may never again, shine as now they shine.
Long before October returns
Seas of blood will have parted us
And you must crush the love in your heart
And I, the love in mine!

The writing and games continued undisturbed until the Reverend Brontë came down with a cold in the summer of 1830. The infection settled in his lungs, and for a time it seemed that he might die. Haworth's minister was too strong-willed to give in to illness, though, and slowly, in the months that followed, he recovered. But being sick taught him that his life could end at any moment, and if he were to die, his children would be left without support.

For this reason, he arranged for fourteen-year-old Charlotte to go to school once more, to be prepared to teach. He sent her to Roe Head, in Mirfield, twenty miles to the southeast. Recommended by Charlotte's godmother, an old family friend named Mrs. Atkinson, Roe Head was known as a clean place that welcomed pupils from respected families. So in January 1831, Charlotte journeyed in a covered cart to Roe Head School.

two

"Bend Inclination to Duty"

AT first, Charlotte felt sick at heart with longing for Haworth. She would steal away when the other girls went out for exercise and sit in the schoolroom's wide bay window, crying for home. One day she thought she was alone, but another homesick new girl had sought privacy in the schoolroom, too. Ellen Nussey approached the tiny figure on the window seat and offered comfort, admitting that she needed consoling in return.

Charlotte found a lifelong friend in pretty, brown-eyed Ellen. She valued Ellen's calm cheerfulness, writing, "When you are a little depressed it does you good to look at Ellen and know she loves you." Charlotte would continue to suffer from spells of depression even after her homesick-ness faded.

"She had ever the demeanour of a born gentlewoman," Ellen said about Charlotte. "She never seemed to me the unattractive little person others designated her." The other girls laughed to themselves when they first saw Charlotte's shabby green dress and crimped, old-womanish hairstyle, and heard the Irish accent she had picked up from her father. Charlotte was thin when she came to Roe Head, Ellen Nussey later recalled, so thin that she seemed "dried in." She looked funny holding books close to her nose, but the girls soon grew used to her, and they learned to admire her quick mind.

Roe Head was a healthier, happier place than the Clergy Daughters' School. It was a school for young ladies, where Miss Margaret Wooler and her four younger sisters taught classes in French, grammar, and geography. Their main purpose, though, was to give the girls a polishing, to make them shine in company and attract worthy husbands. This was why the pupils practiced poise and manners and refined their skills in dancing and music. Most of these girls would never have to teach. Knowing how to draw and do delicate needlework would fill idle hours when they were married and spent most of their time at home, so they perfected these accomplishments, too.

The school drew pupils from nearby industrial towns,

Charlotte Brontë flourished as a student at Roe Head School from January 1831 through June 1832. The schoolroom where she and Ellen Nussey met was on the main floor, on the side of the building that had a bowed exterior.

where their fathers were prosperous mill owners. Their families belonged to the growing middle class that had money enough to stuff its homes with the heavy furniture, draperies, and carpets that were coming into style.

Short, stout Miss Wooler dressed in white. She braided some of her hair into a crown on top of her head and let the rest fall to her shoulders in ringlets. "Bend inclination to duty," she preached to the girls. In other words, a lady must stifle her instincts and do what others expected of her.

Nonsense, declared Charlotte's other new friend, Mary Taylor, who had no intention of obeying this rule. Ellen's friendship gave comfort, but Mary's offered excitement.

Mary was loud and fearless and loved the outdoor games that Charlotte avoided. She was independent and never shy about speaking her mind. Once, when Miss Wooler assigned her a long passage to memorize, Mary refused to do it. She chose to accept her punishment — a month of going to bed without supper — rather than waste time on such a useless task. Mary had vowed never to wed, not as long as a woman's property became her husband's upon marriage. Women were wrong to choose husbands for financial security or a place in society, she believed. She also thought that all professions should be open to women who wanted to pursue them.

Mary had "a fine, generous soul, a noble intellect profoundly cultivated, a heart as true as steel," Charlotte observed. Charlotte, in turn, impressed Mary with the knowledge she had acquired before coming to Roe Head. She knew "things that were out of our range altogether," Mary said.

Studying mattered more than showy accomplishments to Charlotte Brontë, who was preparing to be a governess, not a wife. Her love of learning flourished at Roe Head. "She picked up every scrap of information concerning painting, sculpture, poetry, music, etc., as if it were gold," Mary Taylor recalled. Ellen Nussey added that "she chose in many things to do *double* lessons when not prevented by class arrangement or a companion." Charlotte especially liked learning French. In the evening, she would sit on one of the school's broad window seats, reading by the last rays of light. The other girls wondered how she could see the words with her weak eyes.

Sometimes at night, when the girls should have been going to sleep, Charlotte entertained them by telling stories. Once she invented a tale about a sleepwalker roaming the world and stepping unaware into all kinds of danger. She had him balancing atop castle walls, reaching the edge of a high cliff, and barely avoiding a deep chasm. It was "all told in a voice that conveyed more than words alone

Most Victorian girls were schooled in "accomplishments" rather than knowledge. This young woman has been trained by her teachers to be skilled at needlework. She also plays the harp and paints.

can express," Ellen Nussey remembered. The sleepwalker's next terrifying adventure — standing on a shaky, sky-high tower — proved too much for one listener, a girl who had recently been ill. She started to shiver uncontrollably, and the others had to summon a teacher for help.

The school year was divided into two terms that ended at Christmas and summer. Charlotte went home at the end of each term, but during briefer vacations visited friends from school. Once Branwell escorted Charlotte to the Nussey estate, called The Rydings, where Ellen lived with her widowed mother and sisters and brothers in a great house with turrets like a castle. Charlotte sat beside a brook that flowed through the grounds and walked among ancient chestnut trees that grew nearby. One of the trees had been violently split in two by a powerful bolt of lightning. This stunning picture of nature's power imprinted itself on her mind.

Her brother enjoyed the visit, too. "Branwell," said Ellen, "had probably never been far from home before! He was in wild ecstacy with everything." Branwell "was then a very dear brother, as dear to Charlotte as her own soul: they were in perfect accord of taste and feeling, and it was mutual delight to be together," Ellen observed.

Mary Taylor's home offered different diversions. Called the Red House because it was built of brick, it rang with the voices of six high-spirited children, all close in age. Mary's

Affluent Victorians filled their homes with heavy, dark furniture, curios, and the many decorative items that factories had begun producing for sale.

father was a cultured man who had traveled in Europe. His opinions were as strong as his daughter's, and he loved nothing better than to argue about politics. He sometimes drew Charlotte into the debate, goading her into defending her hero, the Duke of Wellington.

Politeness required Charlotte to visit her godmother and others of her father's friends, but she hated this duty. Her shyness made her afraid to talk, and her small size confused some people. Like other teenagers, Charlotte was eager to appear grown up. She returned to Roe Head furious after one visit because the mistress of the house had treated her like a young child.

Charlotte made such rapid progress that in only eighteen months at Roe Head, she mastered the entire curriculum. She also won the silver medal for proper manners and speech at the end of each term. The medal was a trophy that the winner possessed until the term ended, when another girl might win it. When she left the school in June 1832, Miss Wooler gave her the silver medal to keep. Charlotte went home to Haworth, happy to be living at home again with her brother and sisters.

"In one delightful, though somewhat monotonous course my life is passed," Charlotte wrote to Ellen Nussey about her days back at Haworth. In the morning she taught Emily and Anne. She passed along to them the knowledge she had gained at Roe Head, because they, too, might need to teach for a living one day. The three sisters walked in the afternoon and spent their free time reading, drawing, and adding to the legends of Angria and Gondal. They sought inspiration at night, after their father and aunt went to bed. Then they would silently walk around the dining table, again and again, often arm in arm.

When Ellen visited the Haworth parsonage in July 1833, she saw that Emily and Anne were "inseparable companions." Unlike Charlotte, they never made friends with other girls. They had drawn closer together while Charlotte was away, and a year after her return they remained "in the very closest sympathy which never had any interruption," Ellen said.

Emily, at fifteen, possessed a "lithesome, graceful figure," Ellen observed, and beautiful eyes. "Sometimes they looked grey, sometimes dark blue but she did not often look at you, she was too reserved." Still, Ellen wrote, "One of her rare expressive looks was something to remember throughout life, there was such a *depth* of soul and feeling, and yet shyness of revealing herself, a strength of self-containment seen in no other."

Anne, who was thirteen, "had lovely violet-blue eyes, fine pencilled eye-brows, a clear, almost transparent complexion," according to Ellen. She had curls, like Aunt Branwell, but hers were real, whereas the older woman's were part of a hairpiece.

Ellen learned where Charlotte had acquired her knack for storytelling when she met her friend's father. White-haired and formal, he made sixteen-year-old Ellen shudder and shrink with his "strange stories . . . full of grim humour & interest." The Reverend Brontë told eerie tales about peculiar characters living long ago in forgotten places on the moors. His odd morning habit of firing a pistol out his bedroom window alarmed Ellen even more.

Ellen discovered that the sixth member of this eccentric household, redheaded Branwell, had decided to be a

Anne Brontë, age fourteen, painted by her sister Charlotte.

painter. His father had no doubt that Branwell would become a great artist, so he hired a tutor named William Robinson to come to the parsonage and teach him to paint. Robinson was a successful portrait artist who had painted a number of famous people, including the Duke of Wellington. Charlotte loved the lessons as much as Branwell did, and for a time she spent her days drawing.

Branwell also wanted to write poetry for *Blackwood's Magazine*. He sent letter after letter to the editor, explaining why he should be hired. "I *know* that I am not one of the wretched writers of the day, I know that I possess strength to assist you beyond some of your own contributors," he wrote. He reminded the editor that those contributors were going to die off, and younger writers would need to take their places. "Now Sir, to you I appear writing with conceited assurance, but *I am not*," he stated. "My resolution is to devote my ability to you, and for Gods sake, till you see wether or not I can serve you do not so coldly refuse my aid." The editor never actually refused the brash eighteen-year-old's offer; he simply ignored it.

For Charlotte, the delightful sameness of daily life in Haworth ended in the summer of 1835, when she returned to Miss Wooler's school to teach grammar. It ended as well for Emily, who went with her this time, because the cost of a sister's education was to be part of Charlotte's earnings. Although they were together at Roe Head, neither sister was happy there.

Charlotte hated teaching because it stifled her mind and left her no time to write. "Must I from day to day sit chained to this chair prisoned within these four bare walls, while these glorious summer suns are burning," she wrote in the journal that she kept at this time. Charlotte privately called her pupils "dolts." In her journal she condemned them for lacking imagination. They also demanded too much attention. If she tried to work on her Angrian stories while they did their lessons, they were forever interrupting. On one particular day, her mind had carried her to Africa, where she envisioned a Byronic hero named Zamorna dismounting his black horse. The schoolroom disappeared, and Charlotte stood beneath a sky that was "quivering & shaking with stars." Then she heard an annoying voice calling her back. Africa faded, and she was back at her desk, looking into a pupil's questioning face.

Bending inclination to duty, Charlotte grew depressed. She asked herself, "What in all this is there to remind me of the divine, silent, unseen land of thought, dim now and indefinite as the dream of a dream, the shadow of a shade." Miss Wooler reached out to the despairing teacher, inviting her to talk, but Charlotte rejected her employer's help and chose to be stoical. "I could have been no better company for you than a walking ghost," Charlotte told Miss Wooler.

Emily found the routine of school so stifling that she lasted barely three months at Roe Head. She desperately needed time alone for her creativity to flourish, and she had none at school. She awoke every morning thinking of Haworth and the moorland. These fond thoughts of home darkened even the brightest day for her, and she rapidly wasted away. "Liberty was the breath of Emily's nostrils; without it, she perished," Charlotte said. "I felt in my heart she would die if she did not go home." Charlotte was not about to let Emily follow Maria and Elizabeth into early death, so she arranged for Anne to replace Emily at Roe Head. Anne toiled quietly at her studies, and after a year at school, she earned a medal for good conduct. Anne did her duty by preparing for a governess's life and gave voice to her unhappiness only in poetry:

> *This place of solitude and gloom*
> *Must be my dungeon and my tomb.*
>
> *No hope, no pleasure can I find;*
> *I am grown weary of my mind.*

This year and the next, the Christmas holidays reunited Charlotte and Anne with Branwell and Emily. In late December 1836, Branwell and Charlotte hatched a plan to mail some of their poems to well-known writers and ask for comments and advice. Branwell sent his to William Wordsworth, who wrote so beautifully about nature. Charlotte, meanwhile, wrote to Robert Southey, Britain's poet laureate.

They waited one month, two months, then three, until at last a letter came to the parsonage for Charlotte. It contained advice, but of the kind that could only discourage. Southey had tried his best to destroy Charlotte's dream, and not because she wrote badly. "Literature cannot be

Robert Southey, England's poet laureate from 1813 to 1843, urged Charlotte Brontë to give up writing and pursue a woman's "proper duties."

the business of a woman's life, and it ought not to be," he wrote. "The more she is engaged in proper duties, the less leisure she will have for it, even as an accomplishment and a recreation."

Charlotte Brontë wanted to be a writer more than anything else. How it made her feel to read a statement like this can be guessed from the sarcastic tone of her next letter to Southey. She told him, "I have endeavoured not only attentively to observe all the duties a woman ought to fulfil, but to feel deeply interested in them. I don't always succeed, for sometimes when I'm teaching or sewing I would rather be reading or writing; but I try to deny myself." She concluded, "I trust I shall nevermore feel ambitious to see my name in print; if the wish should rise, I'll look at [your]

letter, and suppress it." Branwell never heard from Wordsworth.

Back at Roe Head, Charlotte struggled against her cre-
ative urges. If she appeared outwardly at peace, she let loose
her frustration in her journal. "Am I to spend all the best
part of my life in this wretched bondage," she asked herself,
"on compulsion assuming an air of kindness, patience &
assiduity?"

While Charlotte fought with herself, Anne grew ill,
and Charlotte and Miss Wooler argued about what to do.
Charlotte wanted to take Anne home, but Miss Wooler
insisted that she was being too cautious. Anne could rest
and recover at Roe Head, Miss Wooler said. Her condition
was hardly grave. At this Charlotte lost her composure.
"I told her one or two rather plain truths, which set her
a-crying," she told Ellen Nussey. As Charlotte prepared
to leave her post, Miss Wooler hurried off a letter to Mr.
Brontë, telling him about the fight.

Tempers cooled, and the two women made up. "If anybody likes me I can't help liking them, and remembering
that she had in general been very kind to me, I gave in
and said I would come back if she wished me," Charlotte
wrote, "but I am not satisfied." Mr. Brontë settled the matter by calling his daughters home. Anne slowly regained
her health at the parsonage, and after the winter holidays,
Charlotte went back to work alone. Sometime before spring

Miss Wooler moved her school to a place called Dewsbury Moor, to a building that was smaller than the one at Roe Head but closer to her own aging father.

"There is a climax to everything, to every state of feeling as well as to every position in life," Charlotte Brontë was later to write. She lasted at Dewsbury Moor until summer neared. Then she decided that her position there and the feelings it evoked had run their course. When she wrote to Ellen Nussey on June 9, she was in Haworth, having left Miss Wooler's school for good, she hoped. "My health and spirits had utterly failed me," Charlotte admitted. "So home I went; the change has at once roused and soothed me — and I am now I trust fairly in the way to be myself again."

A visit from Mary Taylor and her talkative sister Martha added to Charlotte's happiness. "Mary is playing on the piano. Martha is chattering as fast as her little tongue can run and Branwell is standing before her laughing at her vivacity," Charlotte wrote to Ellen, in a letter that sounded like one of the sisters' diary pages.

By the end of July, Branwell had left Haworth to open a portrait studio in Bradford, a center of textile manufacturing. In August, Charlotte reluctantly went back to Dewsbury Moor, and in September 1838, Emily took her first paying job. She was to be a teacher at Law Hill, a ladies'

Branwell Brontë painted this portrait of his sisters. Left to right are Anne, Emily, and Charlotte. The lighter area between Emily and Charlotte is a clue that Branwell's painting once included a fourth person, probably himself, and that he painted over this likeness.

school in Halifax, near Bradford. Only Anne remained at home with their father and aunt.

The young Brontës needed to work. Their father was sixty-one years old, and there was no telling how long he would live, although he took good care of his health. He studied the pages of *Modern Domestic Medicine,* a home-treatment guide, and jotted hundreds of notes in its margins. "Should a flea, or other insect get into the ear — it will produce a dreadful uneasiness — but oil poured in will kill the insect and effect a cure," he wrote. He also noted, "A roasted onion, with a little water and sugar mixed and eaten with bread, is an excellent remedy for a hard dry cough." Still, no one knew when an illness might carry someone away.

three

"WHAT ON EARTH IS HALF SO DEAR?"

MISS Elizabeth Patchett's School, Law Hill, sat high on sloping ground. From the windows of this solid stone mansion, Emily Brontë looked out on a landscape that she loved, miles of farmland and untamed moors. Nearby Halifax offered concerts and art exhibitions that would delight many bright young women. Yet Emily felt downhearted. She complained to Charlotte that she had entered slavery. She was one of three teachers for forty girls ages eleven through fifteen. Miss Patchett had her working from six o'clock in the morning until eleven at night. "I fear she will never stand it," Charlotte wrote to Ellen Nussey.

Emily made it through her first term, "though she

could not easily associate with others," as one of her pupils later reported. According to another girl, Emily told her pupils that she cared more for the school's dog than for any of them. Clearly, Emily, like Charlotte, felt no love for teaching. Her well-being, more than that of her sisters, depended on being in Haworth.

In her brief periods of free time, Emily poured her yearning for home into verses:

There is a spot mid barren hills
Where winter howls and driving rain
But if the dreary tempest chills
There is a light that warms again

The house is old, the trees are bare
And moonless bends the misty dome
But what on earth is half so dear —
So longed for as the hearth of home?

With the start of the second term, Emily looked ahead to bleak winter months. She stopped writing poetry as she fell into despair, and her health deteriorated, as it had at Roe Head. She went home to recover before the term ended. Charlotte had also had enough of the teacher's life. At the end of the fall term in 1838, she told Miss Wooler that she was leaving the school for good, and this time she

Branwell Brontë drew this picture of himself at age twenty-three.

kept her word. For a while, all three sisters were reunited in the parsonage, happily adding to the stories of Angria and Gondal. Branwell came home from Bradford on weekends, either taking a coach or walking the eight miles to Haworth across the moors.

During the week, Branwell occupied a rented room and a studio where he painted portraits of the local clergymen and his landlord's family, the Kirbys. The Kirbys' niece described him as "low in stature, about 5 ft 3 inches high, and slight in build, though well proportioned." She said, "Very few people, except sitters, came to visit him. . . . I recollect his sister Charlotte coming and I remember her sisterly ways." Branwell made friends among the artists and writers of Bradford, who gathered in the George Hotel to talk and joke and drink. He had discovered the pleasures of tavern life, but he gave the Kirbys no cause to complain. Their niece observed, "He was a very steady young gentleman, his conduct was exemplary, and we liked him very much." Despite being liked and having some clients, Branwell earned too little to support himself painting portraits, so sometime in the winter or spring of 1839, he, too, returned to Haworth to live, to his father's great disappointment.

All four of the grown children were then at the parsonage, but for how long? As a young man of twenty-two, Branwell especially needed to launch a career. His attempt to live as a painter had failed, so his father urged him to consider teaching. Father and son embarked on a course of

Charlotte Brontë painted a loving portrait of her closest friend, Ellen Nussey.

study designed to refresh Branwell's knowledge of classical Greek and Latin.

Before long, Branwell's sisters would have to return to teaching—or marry. Being without money and living in such an isolated place, they had slim chances of finding husbands, but marrying still was possible. That same spring, Charlotte received a marriage proposal from Ellen's brother, the Reverend Henry Nussey, age twenty-seven. Henry proposed in a letter, which has been lost, but Charlotte remarked that he wrote "in a common-sense style which does credit to his judgment."

Charlotte had an important decision to make. Henry earned enough money to support a wife, which meant that she would never again have to earn her own way if she accepted him. Because she was unlikely to receive many offers of marriage, this could be her only chance. So she asked herself two questions. First, "Do I love him as much as a woman ought to love the man she marries?" And second, "Am I the person best qualified to make him happy?" The answer to both questions was *no*. She replied to Henry's letter, turning him down. "You do not know me; I am not the serious, grave, cool-headed individual you suppose," she wrote. She ended by saying, "I will never for the sake of attaining the distinction of matrimony and escaping the stigma of an old maid take a worthy man whom I am conscious I cannot render happy." Henry's businesslike proposal could never appeal to a romantic heart like Charlotte's.

Thinking that her friend deserved an explanation, she wrote to Ellen, "I had a kindly leaning towards him because he is an amiable — well-disposed man yet I had not, and never could have that intense attachment which would make me willing to die for him — and if I ever marry it must be in that light of adoration that I will regard my Husband." Henry took Charlotte's refusal in stride. He promptly proposed to another woman, who accepted him, and Charlotte looked forward to an eventual return to teaching.

The next of the four Brontë siblings to try to earn a living was nineteen-year-old Anne. She was hired by a family named Ingham to be their children's governess. The Inghams lived in a mansion near Roe Head called Blake House. They were a prominent family in the region, and their wealth had been passed down for generations. There were five Ingham children in 1839, but Anne had charge of only the oldest boy and girl — Cunliffe, who was six, and Mary, who was five.

Anne had become one of thousands of women employed as governesses in mid-nineteenth-century England. The demand for governesses had grown along with the rising middle class. For as long as people could remember, a chasm that was nearly impossible to cross had separated the upper classes from people in trade. Then, beginning in the 1700s, manufacturing moved from small shops and cottages to factories. The owners of great mills grew wealthier than many aristocrats. And once they had money, they wanted gentility. They dressed like upper-class Britons and mimicked their manners and customs, which included employing governesses to teach their children. A governess became a status symbol for any household hoping to move up.

The social changes spurred by the Industrial Revolution gained momentum after 1837, the year that Queen Victoria took the throne. Victoria's coronation marked the start of the Victorian period, which lasted until 1901, when the queen died. Britain gained power and wealth during Victoria's reign, enlarging and securing its empire of colonies and possessions. The Victorian era was a time of greatness, when the English naturalist Charles Darwin published *On the Origin of Species* and revolutionized people's thinking about evolution. It was the era when an Englishwoman, Florence Nightingale, founded the profession of nursing. Also among the many great British Victorians were Henry Fox Talbot, an inventor of photography, and Alexander Graham Bell, who gave the world the telephone.

The move from home-based production to the factory system had been painful and bloody. Factories employed fewer hands than home looms did and put many weav-

An outstanding figure from the Victorian era, trained nurse Florence Nightingale improved sanitation and patient care at the British army hospital at Üsküdar (in present-day Istanbul) during the Crimean War of the 1850s.

ers out of work in Haworth and elsewhere. International conflict made the problem worse. Great Britain and France were at war, and each was attacking the other's trade. In 1806, Napoleon forbade his European allies from trading with Britain, so in 1807 Great Britain responded with the Orders in Council, prohibiting France from trading with Britain, its allies, and neutral nations. The Royal Navy enforced the orders by blockading French ports. Reduced foreign trade meant less work, and lower profits, for large and small manufacturers in England.

As their families starved, some displaced workers

struck out violently. Beginning in 1811, in Yorkshire and other manufacturing centers, bands of men descended on mills to destroy the power looms and knitting frames that had taken away their livelihood. They called themselves Luddites in recognition of their unseen leader, Ned Ludd, who might have been real or imaginary. The government sent in thousands of armed foot soldiers and cavalrymen to halt the rioting and destruction. By the end of the decade, the forces of law and order had snuffed out the Luddite movement and hanged its ringleaders or deported them to Australia.

Later, during the Victorian period, needy people seeking work moved from the English countryside to the slums that were growing around cities. There, factories devoured their hard labor and paid them barely enough to get by. Fueled by coal, the mighty factories spewed out smoke that darkened the sky, choked plant life, and even blackened the wool of sheep.

In fine homes supported by this system, governesses instructed their charges in "the usual branches of a solid English education," which included reading, spelling, and a modern foreign language, usually French. A governess might also give instruction in music, drawing, dancing, and fancy needlework. Perhaps most important, she was to set an example of high moral standards and proper behavior. Governesses came from groups that enjoyed social stature but lacked money. They were unmarried daughters of clergymen, military officers, and aristocrats who had lost their fortunes.

According to Charlotte, Anne wrote home to say that her pupils were "desperate little dunces"—dolts in the making—and beyond her control. Anne's employers had ordered her not to punish the children, but to inform Mrs. Ingham if they misbehaved. There was one big problem with this system: The children knew their mother would be lenient, so they had no reason to obey their governess. Anne scolded them uselessly, and she tried methods that would be called inappropriate today. Once, she tied Cunliffe and Mary to a table leg to make them do their lessons. Anne rightly felt that her employers gave her no support, but she also showed little understanding of children. Years later, Mrs. Ingham commented that she "had once employed a very unsuitable governess called Miss Brontë."

Charlotte, too, tried her luck as a governess. In May 1839, she took a temporary job with a family named Sidgwick, whose great home, Stonegappe, was twelve miles from Haworth. She was to teach and care for the two youngest Sidgwick children, seven-year-old Matilda and four-year-old John Benson. At first Charlotte, like Anne, found the children impossible to govern. "More riotous, perverse, unmanageable cubs never grew," she griped. On one occasion, John Benson threw a rock at Charlotte and hit her on the head. Nevertheless, unlike Anne, Charlotte won over the children well enough to enjoy order in the schoolroom.

But she never adjusted to her place in the household. Charlotte had known of Mrs. Sidgwick before her marriage, when she was Hannah Greenwood of Keighley, the daughter of a cotton manufacturer. She expected to be greeted as an equal and given the respect owed to her as the Reverend Brontë's daughter. Instead, Mrs. Sidgwick treated Charlotte almost like a stranger. Charlotte wrote to Emily that her employer "does not intend to know me." Charlotte took

A governess enjoyed little respect, even from the children in her care. The boys in this family clearly want to escape the home schoolroom, and one refuses to study at all.

care of the children from morning until night. Once they were asleep, she had to work on the mountain of sewing that Mrs. Sidgwick had given her to do.

A governess like Charlotte held an awkward place in England's complex social structure. As a minister's daughter, she came from a higher class than her employers, who had earned their money in trade. Yet no true lady worked, so by taking a job she had lowered herself socially. There was one standard for men and another for women, as the English writer Sarah Stickney Ellis explained: "Gentlemen may employ their hours of business in almost any degrading occupation and . . . may be gentlemen still; while, if a

A book is this sad, lonely governess's only friend.

lady but touch any article, no matter how delicate, in the way of trade, she loses caste and ceases to be a lady."

A governess was forbidden to have suitors or to show affection to her pupils. She was to wear drab clothes to avoid attracting the notice of unmarried uncles, older brothers, and even straying husbands. "She may be known from her plain and quiet style of dress; a deep straw bonnet with green or brown veil and on her face a fixed sad look of despair," noted a ladies' magazine from 1840.

Charlotte complained about the Sidgwicks, but they found fault with her as well. They thought she was too touchy. She became angry if the Sidgwicks asked her to walk to church with them, because she thought they were ordering her around. Yet if they failed to invite her, she sulked about being ignored. Then, if a spell of depression fell on her, she would spend the day in bed, leaving the pregnant Mrs. Sidgwick to do her work. It was fortunate for both Charlotte and the Sidgwicks that the regular governess returned in July.

Upon coming home, Charlotte received a second proposal of marriage. This one came from David Bryce, an Irish clergyman, who asked her to marry him after visiting the Haworth parsonage and meeting her only once. Charlotte turned him down, and the unlucky Mr. Bryce died several months later. "I am tolerably well convinced that I shall never marry at all," Charlotte confided to Ellen Nussey.

Before the weather turned cold, two of the Brontës did some traveling. Branwell and a friend took a sightseeing trip to the busy port of Liverpool, on the Irish Sea. Liverpool "owes its fame to its commerce," decided a writer of Branwell's time. Every day, ships left Liverpool carrying the products of English factories to foreign buyers. Other ships arrived from the New World with tobacco, rice, sugar, and rum. Passenger vessels came and went as well, transporting people to and from North America. Branwell was bothered by a facial tic during this trip and took opium to relax his muscles. Opium was legal and easy to find in nineteenth-century England, where people used it as a medicine.

Charlotte had a bigger adventure when she and Ellen Nussey went to the eastern seaside resort of Bridlington. Charlotte had never been to the seashore and was enthralled with "the idea of seeing the SEA—of being near it," and watching things she had only read about, "its changes by sunrise, Sunset—moonlight—& noonday—in calm—perhaps in storm." The two friends went by train, which was still a new way to travel, and by horse-drawn coach. The sea was mightier and more magnificent than Charlotte could have imagined. When she and Ellen first walked to the shore, she stood there silently, in tears. "Its glorious changes—its ebb and flow—the sound of its restless waves—formed a subject for Contemplation that never wearied either the eye, the ear, or the mind," she commented.

Charlotte and Branwell spent the autumn and early winter with Emily, writing stories and poems. When Anne came home for Christmas, she informed her family that she would not be going back to the Inghams in the new year; she had been dismissed. The Brontë sisters were completely unsuited for teaching and caring for children, in Ellen Nussey's opinion. "There never could have been temperaments *less adapted* to such a position," she concluded. When Tabby Aykroyd, the family's longtime servant, fell and broke her leg, the sisters busily nursed her themselves. They took over Tabby's household chores and threw themselves into this new work. Emily, who loved the kitchen, did all the cooking and baking; Anne oversaw the housecleaning; and Charlotte did the ironing, although she burned several garments before she got the knack of it.

The sisters also spent the last days of December sewing shirts for Branwell, who had been hired as a tutor for two boys, ages eleven and ten. They were the stepsons of Robert Postlethwaite, a landowner living in the Lake District, near the poet William Wordsworth. The Postlethwaite family had made its money building ships and selling timber. On December 31, Branwell said goodbye to his family and took a coach to the town of Kendal, where he bade "farewell of old friend whisky," as he told his pal John Brown. Brown was the Reverend Brontë's sexton, the man who maintained the church building and graveyard.

The farewell was temporary, because upon reaching the Lake District, Branwell joined a group of men drinking at the Royal Hotel. Before the wild night was over, an Irish squire and "a native of the land of Israel" got into a barroom brawl. Branwell joined the fight on the side of Ireland and reported that "a regular rumpus ensued." He bragged, "I found myself in bed next morning with a bottle of porter, a glass, and a corkscrew beside me." That day he went on to Broughton, where the Postlethwaites lived.

Branwell made a good first impression, as he reported to John Brown: "I take neither spirits, wine nor malt liquors, I dress in black and smile like a saint or martyr. Everybody says, 'what a good young Gentleman is Mr Postlethwaite's tutor!'" Branwell lodged in the town, so when he was not teaching, his time was his own. He took long rambles in the countryside, which he loved to do, and he again sent his writing to poets, asking for advice.

He was thrilled to get a letter back from the writer Hartley Coleridge, the author of biographies and poems. Coleridge's father, Samuel Taylor Coleridge, was one of the great English Romantic poets, known for writing mystical, symbolic works like *The Rime of the Ancient Mariner* and *Kubla Khan*. The younger Coleridge's letter has been lost, but in it he invited Branwell to his home, Nab Cottage. Branwell made this visit on May 1; after spending a day with Hartley Coleridge, he returned to his room to translate Homer's *Odes* from classical Greek into English. Coleridge had promised to read Branwell's translation when it was finished.

Life seemed to be going well for Branwell until Mr. Postlethwaite fired him two months later. No one knows for certain why Branwell lost his job. He may have been spending too much time writing poetry and not enough time teaching. Or he may have made too many trips to the tavern, despite his boast of being sober. He did remark that his landlord, a Mr. Fish, was drunk "two days out of every seven." Also, some years later, a local nobleman wrote in his commonplace book, or notebook, that Branwell was dismissed for having an affair with a woman in his employer's house, which led to a pregnancy. The woman was either a daughter or a servant, and the child, born months after Branwell had gone, later died. Whatever the reason for his firing, Branwell packed up his things and headed for home, having failed again.

Emboldened by Branwell's successful contact with Hartley Coleridge, Charlotte sent Coleridge a portion of a novel that she had started. She signed her letter "C.T.," to keep her identity a secret and to prevent Coleridge from knowing whether she was a woman or a man. She wanted to be judged simply as a writer. But, like Robert Southey, Coleridge offered this eager writer no encouragement.

While Branwell was away, his sisters had been enjoying the company of another young man. All the Brontës liked handsome William Weightman, who came to Haworth to be the Reverend Brontë's curate. A curate serves as an assistant to a priest or minister. Curates are often young, newly ordained, and in training to lead their own congregations one day. Weightman was "agreeable in person and manners, and constitutionally cheerful," Patrick Brontë observed. "His character wore well." The families of Haworth also grew fond of the kindly curate who baptized their children, buried their dead, and called on their sick and lonely.

Charlotte Brontë sketched the good-natured William Weightman.

Weightman's gentle teasing of Aunt Branwell made the Brontë sisters laugh. Charlotte playfully called him "Miss Celia Amelia Weightman." She decided to sketch his portrait and had him pose in his clerical gown.

Acting anonymously, Weightman sent the three women their very first valentines, each with verses written for its recipient. Charlotte, Emily, and Anne knew right away who had sent these charming love notes. They put their heads together and wrote a poem for him in return:

> *Believe us when we frankly say*
> *(Our words, though blunt are true),*
> *At home, abroad, by night or day,*
> *We all wish well for you.*
>
> *And never may a cloud come o'er*
> *The sunshine of your mind;*
> *Kind friends, warm hearts, and happy hours,*
> *Through life we trust you'll find.*

Weightman playfully flirted with all three sisters, but he may have felt most attracted to Anne. Charlotte remarked in one of her letters to Ellen that the curate "sits opposite to Anne at church sighing softly and looking out of the corners of his eyes to win her attention — And Anne is so quiet, her look so downcast — they are a picture."

No romance developed, however, because Anne left the happy circle in May 1840 to be a governess again. She was to teach four children, three girls and a boy, in the Robinson family, near the city of York. The Robinsons' estate was called Thorp Green. Their mansion was more than twice the size of the Inghams' home, and they needed a large staff of servants to run it. Born into wealth, Mr. Edmund Robinson was a minister, but chronic ill health kept him away from the pulpit. His wife, Lydia Robinson, was dark haired and full of life.

Branwell, too, tried again to make his way in the world. In autumn 1840 he went to work for the Leeds and Manchester Railway. He was assigned to the station in Sowerby, a bustling textile-manufacturing town near Halifax. The station was brand-new, and the railroad line would not be complete until work finished on the 1.6-mile Summit Tunnel, which runs beneath the Pennine Mountains of northern England. Then the longest railroad tunnel in the world, the Summit Tunnel represented speed and progress.

As an assistant clerk, Branwell kept a record of the trains that stopped at the Sowerby station and the freight they carried. He also looked out for passengers' safety. Charlotte thought that this low-level job was beneath her brother's ability, but railroads were expanding, and Branwell looked forward to being promoted. Indeed, after six months he rose to clerk-in-charge of the Luddendenfoot Station and received a raise.

At this time Branwell befriended Francis Grundy, a young man he could impress with his knowledge and talent. Grundy described Branwell as "small and thin of person" and "the reverse of attractive at first sight." Branwell "had a mass of red hair, which he wore high off his forehead — to help his height, I fancy; a great, bumpy, intellectual forehead, nearly half the size of the whole facial contour; small ferrety eyes, deep sunk, and still further hidden by the never removed spectacles."

Then, as always happened with Branwell, something went wrong. In March 1842, the railroad's auditors looked at his account books and discovered that money was missing. Branwell had lost more than eleven pounds, a little more than he earned in a month. No one accused him of stealing the money, but it had been his job to keep track of it, so Branwell was fired once more.

four

"WHO EVER ROSE . . . WITHOUT AMBITION?"

*S*HORTLY before Branwell moved to Luddendenfoot, Charlotte tried once more to be a governess. She worked for the family of a merchant named John White, teaching and caring for a girl and boy, ages eight and six. She still had mounds of sewing to do, but the White children behaved better than the young Sidgwicks had. Their parents treated Charlotte kindly, giving her time off to visit Ellen and offering to let her father spend time at their home. They even said yes when Charlotte asked to extend her summer holiday from one week to three.

None of this mattered to Charlotte, who had made up her mind to hate her new job. "No one but myself can tell how hard a governess's work is to me," she declared, "for no one but myself is aware how utterly averse my whole mind and nature are to employment."

That summer, when Anne and Charlotte spent their holidays at home, the sisters devised a plan to free themselves from working for others. As Emily wrote in a diary paper on her twenty-third birthday, "A scheme is at present in agitation for setting us up in a school of our own." Aunt Branwell was to lend her nieces money to rent a building and equip it as a school for girls. Miss Wooler even offered to let them take over the school at Dewsbury Moor, which would lower the cost of starting up.

On the same day that Emily wrote her diary paper, Anne wondered "what will be our condition and how or where shall we all be on this day four years hence." Emily, thinking along the same lines, imagined the sisters "all merrily seated in our own sitting-room in some pleasant and flourishing seminary."

Then Charlotte found a better way to use some of Aunt Branwell's money. Her unconventional friend, Mary Taylor, was studying with her sister, Martha, in Brussels, Belgium, where their uncle Abraham lived. Mary urged Charlotte to do the same, but Charlotte needed little coaxing. Here was a chance to travel, to live far from home amid new sights and faces. Here was an opportunity to learn! With luck, the teachers in Brussels would challenge her eager mind.

"Papa will perhaps think it a wild and ambitious scheme;" but, Charlotte asked, "who ever rose in the world without ambition?" This statement would have shocked many people, because for a woman to be ambitious went against the Victorian ideal. Still, Charlotte boldly admitted that when her father left Ireland to go to Cambridge University, "he was as ambitious as I am now."

To persuade her father and aunt, Charlotte stressed the practical side of the venture. Spending time abroad refining her French would make Charlotte stand out from the many other Englishwomen running schools, she said. Also, in Brussels she might meet Belgian families wanting to educate their daughters in England and recruit these girls as pupils. The Reverend Brontë and Aunt Branwell agreed to the plan, to Charlotte's great joy. It was decided that Emily would study with Charlotte in Brussels while Anne remained with the Robinsons.

As far as their father and aunt knew, Emily and Charlotte would be gone for six months. But Charlotte whispered to Emily, "Before our half year in Brussels is completed, you and I will have to seek employment abroad."

The Reverend Brontë escorted his daughters, although they traveled as well with Mary Taylor, who had made a brief trip to England, and her brother Joe. Together this group went by boat to the Belgian port of Ostend and journeyed inland past fertile plains. Mounting a hill, they saw in the distance the towers and steeples of the Belgian capital.

The Taylors' school was too costly for the Brontës, so Charlotte and Emily had chosen instead the Pensionnat Heger, a girls' boarding school in the old part of Brussels. The long, low school building appeared unadorned and even grim when viewed from the narrow cobblestone street, but it had a pleasant, well-tended garden hidden from view. Once inside the door, the sisters received a warm greeting. The director, Madame Claire Zoë Heger, lived at

Students pose in the garden of the Pensionnat Heger. This photograph was taken in 1883, some years after Charlotte and Emily Brontë left the school.

the school with her children and husband, Monsieur Constantin Heger, who taught literature to the girls. He and the other teachers taught exclusively in French, one of Belgium's principal languages. (Flemish and German are the other two.)

Constantin Heger, age thirty-three, was "a little black ugly being," Charlotte observed. He might have been "a man of power as to mind," but he was "irritable in temperament." Another student recalled, "In talking perhaps he made his profoundest impression by a steadfast often mocking gaze."

This forceful teacher quickly noted that his two new students had unusual ability. He saw how much Charlotte loved to learn. He recommended books for her to read, and he reviewed her compositions with extra care. He taught her to improve her writing, telling her to "sacrifice, *without pity,* everything that does not contribute to clarity." He spurred her on to find *le mot juste* — exactly the right word to express what she wanted to say.

Monsieur, as he was called, would read to the sisters from works by great French authors. After discussing a passage, he would ask them to write — in French — a composition of their own, sometimes inspired by the famous author's subject or words. Charlotte accepted the challenge. Under Monsieur's direction, she also wrote on religious topics like "the Death of Moses" or "the Immensity of God." In a paper titled "The Nest," a subject of her own choosing, she described how watching a mother bird tending her hatchlings had revealed God's presence. She wrote, "The bird's nest is but a line, a word in the huge book that Nature opens for the instruction of the entire human race, a book whose every page abounds with proof of the existence of God."

Emily refused to write like anyone but herself. It was her own idea to write about King Harold, who died defending England from Norman invaders in 1066. She breathed life into this ancient king who was transformed into a hero by war:

> He is inwardly convinced that a mortal power will not fell him. The hand of Death, alone, can bear the victory away from his arms, and Harold is ready to succumb before it, because the touch of that hand is, to the hero, what the stroke that gave him liberty was to the slave.

Monsieur Heger gave Emily more freedom in her studies than he allowed the other students, because he saw that she had an extraordinary mind. She possessed "a head for logic, and a capability of argument" that were "rare indeed in a woman," he said. He knew only one way to make sense of Emily's intelligence: "She should have been a man." Emily had come to the school knowing very little French, so she had to study hard at first to keep up with Charlotte and the others, but she made rapid progress. "Emily works like a horse," Charlotte noted.

In the past, leaving home had caused Emily's health to break down, and Charlotte worried that this might happen again in Brussels. In fact, it looked for a while as though Emily might be sinking. Charlotte felt relieved, before long, to see that "this time she rallied through the mere force of resolution."

Emily insisted on wearing the old-fashioned hand-sewn clothes that she brought from home. They were as good as anything else, she thought. Her dresses had full, puffy sleeves that had been out of style for a decade or more. She hated petticoats, so her skirts clung strangely to her long legs. Clearly, Emily gave little thought to her appearance. "I wish to be as God made me," she simply said. Charlotte, more willing to conform, learned from the Belgian girls at school to wear embroidered collars and tailor her dresses to flatter her small frame.

By July 1842, as the sisters' six months in Brussels neared their end, Madame Heger invited them to stay for another half year. There was no need to worry about tuition, because they could earn their keep by teaching, she said; Charlotte could teach English, and Emily, who had musical talent, might give piano lessons. Mary Taylor thought they were quite right to accept Madame's offer. She remarked that Charlotte and Emily looked well, "not only in health but in mind & hope. They are content with their present position & even gay."

Emily's first pupils were English girls, three young sisters from a family named Wheelwright. She made enemies of these girls right away by insisting they have lessons during their playtime. She needed the other hours in the day for her own studies, she claimed. "I simply disliked her from the first," said the girls' older sister Laetitia. The Wheelwrights liked Charlotte and would have invited her to their home — if not for Emily. "Charlotte was so devotedly attached to her, and thought so highly of her talents, that it would only have caused offence to exclude her sister," Laetitia Wheelwright said.

Emily thought that friendship wasted her time. At the Hegers' school she made only one friend, a sixteen-year-old Belgian girl named Louise de Bassompierre. Unlike everyone else at the school, Louise found Emily easier to approach than Charlotte. Emily gave Louise a pencil drawing that she had done of a weather-torn pine tree, and Louise treasured this gift for years.

Charlotte was friendlier to most people than Emily was,

but not much. She looked down on her Belgian classmates, believing them duller than English girls. She enjoyed visiting the Taylor sisters at their school, yet she appeared shy and strange to the other English people she met in Brussels. For a while a Reverend and Mrs. Jenkins of the British embassy invited Emily and Charlotte for Sunday and holiday visits, but the sisters seemed uneasy in their home. Charlotte turned away and hid her face if anyone spoke to her. Emily, even more aloof, barely said a word. "We are completely isolated in the midst of numbers," Charlotte wrote to Ellen Nussey, but the isolation was largely their own fault.

The most important friendship that Charlotte formed in Belgium was with Monsieur. Before long, their relationship as student and teacher grew into feelings of deep regard. If Charlotte raised the lid of her desk and smelled the aroma of Monsieur's cigar, she knew that he had left a book in there for her to find.

The new school term had barely begun when a letter came from England bearing bad news. Charlotte and Emily learned that their charming friend, the curate William Weightman, had died of cholera. Long known and feared in tropical places, cholera had migrated through Europe in the early nineteenth century. It reached Britain in 1831 and moved quickly into cities and villages. No one knew

Constantin Heger, shown here in later life, recognized the talent of Charlotte and Emily Brontë. He and Charlotte became friends, and she grew to love him.

that bacteria caused cholera, or that it was spread through contaminated water, so no one knew how to prevent it. Most victims died of dehydration, often quickly. Cholera caused such violent diarrhea that water seemed to pour out of a sufferer's body. Skin sagged; eyes sank into the head; the face turned blue; hands lay shriveled and wasted.

Weightman caught this terrible disease while visiting the poor and sick of Haworth. Young and strong, he fought off death for two weeks. The Brontë men visited him in his illness, although Branwell fell to pieces in sorrow. The Reverend Brontë remained strong, however. He prayed with the dying curate and listened to what was on his mind. When the time came, the older man "saw him in tranquility close his eyes on this bustling, vain, selfish world." Moreover, "I may truly say," he concluded, "his end was peace, and his hope glory."

Anne, still working for the Robinsons at Thorp Green, wrote a poem comparing Weightman's brief, sunny life to a dazzling morning cut short by clouds and rain. She consoled herself with the thought that:

> *If few and short the joys of life*
> *That thou on earth couldst know,*
> *Little thou knew'st of sin and strife*
> *Nor much of pain and woe.*
> . . . .
> *And yet I cannot check my sighs,*
> *Thou wert so young and fair,*
> *More bright than summer morning skies,*
> *But stern death would not spare.*

The people of Haworth had so loved Weightman that they paid for a monument to him that was placed in the church. Its inscription praised Weightman's "orthodox principles, active zeal, moral habits, learning, mildness, and affability," as well as "his useful labours."

Martha Taylor, Mary's sister, became the next young person to die unexpectedly, after contracting an illness that most likely also was cholera. Throughout Martha's sickness, Mary "was to her more than a mother—more than a sister: watching, nursing, cherishing her so tenderly, so unweariedly," Charlotte informed Ellen Nussey. Martha died on October 12, at age twenty-three, and was buried in the Protestant cemetery in Brussels. Charlotte and Emily walked with Mary to see Martha's grave, and Charlotte told Ellen that their friend was coming to terms with her sorrow. Mary appeared "calm and serious now." There were no more "bursts of violent emotion, no exaggeration of distress." Mary arranged to go to Germany to teach English at a school for boys. This was a daring move; for a lady to instruct schoolboys went against the accepted rules of propriety in England. Miss Wooler heard about Mary's plan from Ellen, and she disapproved.

As Mary made ready to leave, another letter from Haworth told Emily and Charlotte that Aunt Branwell was ill and near death. The sisters left for home immediately. They hoped to see for one last time the woman who had devoted her life to their care, but this was not to be. They reached the parsonage on November 2, just missing Aunt's funeral. She had died painfully of a blocked intestine on October 29.

A similar letter had brought Anne home from the Robinsons, so for a few weeks the Brontës were together in their grief. Branwell, the most emotional, felt the loss most keenly. The moans of his dying aunt's nighttime suffering played over and over in his brain. "I have now lost the

guide and director of all the happy days connected with my childhood," he lamented to his friend Francis Grundy.

Aunt Branwell left each of the four young Brontës a personal memento. Her money was divided equally among her four nieces: Charlotte, Emily, Anne, and their cousin Eliza Kingston, who lived far to the south in Cornwall. Each received a little less than three hundred pounds. It was hardly a fortune, but it would be some insurance against poverty. Aunt had assumed that Branwell would be better able to earn a decent living, because he was a man.

But would he? After being fired from his railroad job, Branwell had struggled through a period of drinking, opium use, illness, and deep depression. It was *"almost insanity,"* he wrote. Gradually his mind and body healed, and by May he was telling Grundy, "I can now speak cheerfully and enjoy the company of another without the stimulus of six glasses of whisky." He would have recovered sooner, he claimed, if he had something to do.

Branwell had been writing, and he had managed to publish some poems in local newspapers. Most were old Angrian poems that he had revised, but he also published the first section of a new poem. It was a long saga that began with Noah speaking at the grave of Methuselah, the oldest person mentioned in the Old Testament:

> *Shall this pale Corpse whose hoary hairs*
> *Are just surrendered to decay*
> *Dissolve the chain that bound our years*
> *To hundred ages past away?*
> . . . .
> *Shall that dark doom which hangs oer head*
> *Its blinded victims darker find? —*
> *Shall storms from Heaven without the world*
> *Find wilder storms from Hell within?*

It was Anne who found Branwell something more to do. Edmund Robinson, Jr., her employers' only son, had grown too old for a governess, so Anne persuaded the Robinsons to hire Branwell as his tutor. When she returned to Thorp Green after Christmas to continue on as governess to the girls, Branwell came along to teach young Edmund.

Branwell Brontë sketched Thorp Green, the home of the Robinsons, who employed both Branwell and Anne.

Charlotte, still in England, was glad to see Ellen Nussey, but her thoughts kept drifting across the Strait of Dover, to Belgium. She felt "an irresistible impulse," she said, to get back to the Pensionnat Heger, to the teacher who saw and appreciated her talent. Emily had spent enough time abroad, though. She chose to remain in the parsonage, where she was happiest, and take Aunt's place as her father's housekeeper.

Aunt Branwell's death gave Charlotte greater freedom. As a respectable lady of an earlier generation, Miss Branwell never would have made a long trip alone. She certainly never would have let her niece go from Haworth to Brussels without a chaperone. Charlotte, more modern in her thinking, had no fear of traveling unescorted. She said goodbye to her dear friend Ellen Nussey with a joke: "It seems you will hardly hear me — all the waves of the Channel, heaving & roaring between must deaden the sound." She took a train from Leeds to London, a journey of thirteen hours. After being left by a cab driver on London's wharf at night, she argued with the crew of the boat that was to carry her to Belgium in the morning. It was against company policy to let passengers aboard on the night before departure, but Charlotte refused to be left standing alone and unprotected in a dangerous place. She won the fight and was allowed to go on.

Back in Brussels, Charlotte took over the teaching of English at the Hegers' school. The couple welcomed her into their sitting room as a friend when the school day ended, and she resumed her private studies with Monsieur. She began using her essays to speak from her heart to the teacher who held her in such high esteem. In a composition titled "Letter from a Poor Painter to a Great Lord," she allowed the fictional painter to voice her own words, revealing thoughts that she had never dared confide to another:

Throughout my early youth the difference that existed between myself and most of the people around me was, for me, an embarrassing enigma that I did not know how to resolve. . . . I believed it my duty to follow the example set by the majority of my acquaintances . . . yet all the while I felt myself incapable of feeling and acting as they felt and acted. . . . In vain I tried to imitate the gentle gaiety, the serene and even temper, that I saw in the faces of my companions and found so worthy of admiration; all my efforts were useless. I could not restrain the ebb and flow of blood in my arteries, and that ebb and flow left its mark upon my . . . hard and unengaging features; I cried in secret.

Charlotte's affection for Monsieur Heger was deepening into love. She tried through her writing to draw him closer and make him admire her all the more. Monsieur kept up his side of the friendship and continued to present her with books. Then, after two happy months, the atmosphere changed at the Pensionnat Heger. Madame stopped inviting Charlotte into the sitting room. The private lessons ended, and Monsieur counseled Charlotte to practice *bienveillance,* or kindness, by making friends with the other teachers, women she disliked and snubbed. Charlotte was sure that Madame had made her husband say these things.

It seems that Madame Heger had noticed Charlotte's warm feelings for her husband and was determined to cool them. She withdrew her friendship and treated the Eng-

On a letter to Ellen Nussey, Charlotte Brontë drew herself looking small and homely, and calling goodbye to her friend and a suitor on the other side of the English Channel.

lish teacher with distant formality. How deeply Constantin Heger cared for Charlotte Brontë can only be guessed. He admired her mind, but, if readers can believe a gentleman who knew the Hegers, he never returned her passion. "He was a worshipper of intellect & he worshipped Charlotte Bronte thus far & no further," wrote this man, who had seen Monsieur Heger single out another bright girl for attention.

The cloud of depression settled again over Charlotte Brontë. It grew thicker and blacker as August neared and the school closed for five weeks of summer holiday. The Hegers, the other teachers, the pupils — just about everyone left for vacation while Charlotte stayed at the *pensionnat* nearly alone. Day after day, she wandered along the streets of Brussels, a solitary figure. She walked to the Protestant cemetery to see Martha Taylor's grave. Once, loneliness drove her into a Catholic church, where she confessed her sins to a priest, although as a member of the Church of England, she was a Protestant. "I actually did confess — a real confession," she disclosed to Emily. The priest hearing Charlotte's sins invited her to come for instruction in the Catholic faith, but she never went.

The five weeks passed, and as the autumn term began, Charlotte gave up her plan of living and working abroad. Monsieur pressured her to stay, but Mary Taylor agreed that it was time for Charlotte to leave the Hegers. Mary invited her friend to join her as a teacher at the German school, but Charlotte declined the offer. She had admitted

Charlotte Brontë offered up her confession at the Cathedral of St. Gudule in Brussels.

to being ambitious; she had defied convention and traveled to a foreign country alone; but to be a woman teaching adolescent boys was too radical a step even for Charlotte Brontë to take. She labored on at her post through December, when Monsieur gave her a diploma as proof of her ability to teach. On January 1, Madame Heger went with Charlotte as far as the port of Ostend and made sure the lonesome, lovesick teacher boarded the boat for home.

five

"A Peculiar Music"

I SUFFERED much before I left Brussels," Charlotte Brontë confided to Ellen Nussey, her closest friend. "I think, however long I live, I shall not forget what parting with M. Heger cost me." Charlotte kept up with her studies by memorizing a passage in French every day. Once every two weeks, she allowed herself the delicious treat of writing a letter to Monsieur. She then waited anxiously for his reply.

The correspondence went on in this way until Madame Heger found three of Charlotte's letters that Monsieur had torn up and tossed into a wastebasket. She treated these scraps like puzzle pieces, painstakingly matching their edges to discover what Charlotte had written. "Oh it is certain that I shall see you again one day," she read; "it must be so — for as soon as I have earned enough money to go to Brussels I will go there — and I will see you again even if it is only for a moment." Before confronting her husband, Madame stitched two of the letters back together, and she repaired the third with strips of paper and glue. Presenting the evidence, she told Monsieur that if he and Charlotte were determined to stay in touch, they must each write no more than one letter every six months.

As soon as I have earned enough money . . . The only way to make money that stood open to Charlotte Brontë was teaching, but she lacked the heart to leave home and work in some school, or to hire herself out as a governess again. So she returned to the idea of opening a girls' boarding school, this time in the Haworth parsonage. It would be a

Charlotte Brontë drew these trees growing toward each other to represent herself and Constantin Heger. Charlotte mailed the drawing to Monsieur.

small school, with five or six pupils sleeping in the rooms that Branwell and Anne had vacated. Charlotte would do most of the teaching, and Emily would keep house. Charlotte had cards printed, advertising "The Misses Brontë's Establishment" and listing the fees. She sent them to friends and acquaintances, including Ellen, who was to distribute them in Dewsbury.

Despite everyone's best efforts, not a single family inquired about sending a daughter to the Brontës' school. Haworth was simply too remote and hard to reach. Its isolation outweighed Charlotte's outstanding qualifications in every parent's opinion, so the planned school failed before it could open.

It was just as well, because in June 1845, Anne unexpectedly came home, and Branwell followed not long after. Anne quit her job with the Robinsons after she "had some very unpleasant and undreamt-of experience of human nature," she wrote. Anne left no further explanation for her departure. Branwell, according to Charlotte, had been fired for proceedings that were "bad beyond expression," and he was forbidden to have further contact with any member of the Robinson family.

The facts came out in Branwell's letters to his friends: he had carried on a love affair with Lydia Robinson, his employer's spirited wife. While still at Thorp Green, he had informed John Brown, "My mistress is DAMNABLY

The Misses Brontë's Establishment

FOR

THE BOARD AND EDUCATION

OF A LIMITED NUMBER OF

YOUNG LADIES,

THE PARSONAGE, HAWORTH,

NEAR BRADFORD.

Terms.

	£.	s.	d.
BOARD AND EDUCATION, including Writing, Arithmetic, History, Grammar, Geography, and Needle Work, per Annum,	35	0	0
French, German, Latin — each per Quarter,	1	1	0
Music, Drawing — each per Quarter,	1	1	0
Use of Piano Forte, per Quarter,	0	5	0
Washing, per Quarter,	0	15	0

Each Young Lady to be provided with One Pair of Sheets, Pillow Cases, Four Towels, a Dessert and Tea-spoon.

A Quarter's Notice, or a Quarter's Board, is required previous to the Removal of a Pupil.

Charlotte and Emily advertised "The Misses Brontë's Establishment" and offered lessons in French, German, Latin, music, and drawing. No students applied.

TOO FOND OF ME." From Haworth, he wrote to Francis Grundy that Mrs. Robinson's kindness had "ripened into declarations of more than ordinary feeling." His admiration for her "mental and personal attractions" had grown into "an attachment on my part, and led to reciprocations which I had little looked for." Mr. Robinson learned of the affair and fired the guilty tutor.

Feeling wronged more than ashamed, Branwell drank

away his sorrow in taverns night after night, or sought peace through opium. He begged money from his family, raged against his fate, and became more than flesh and blood could bear. "No one in the house could have rest," Charlotte complained. Hoping to restore Branwell's mind and healthy habits, the Brontës sent him off with his friend John Brown to Liverpool and the Welsh coast. The change of scene may have helped Branwell control his outbursts, but he complained that wherever he went, "a certain woman robed in black, and calling herself 'MISERY,' walked by my side, and leant on my arm as affectionately as if she were my legal wife."

Emily and Anne found some calm by taking a short train trip to the city of York. Twenty-seven and twenty-five years old, they still loved to lose themselves in Gondal fantasies. Emily wrote in a diary paper:

> *During our excursion we were, Ronald Macalgin, Henry Angora, Juliet Angusteena, Rosabella Esmaldan, Ella and Julian Egremont, Catharine Navarre, and Cordelia Fitzaphnold, escaping from the palaces of instruction to join the Royalists who are hard driven at present by the victorious Republicans.*

To Charlotte, who was secretly dealing with her own impossible love, life in the parsonage was depressing. Again

Mary Taylor urged her to get away. "I told her very warmly that she ought not to stay at home," Mary said, "that to spend the next five years at home, in solitude and weak health, would ruin her." Mary had left the German school and was soon to sail to the other side of the world, to the young British colony of New Zealand. A book for new settlers claimed that no place on Earth offered "a more promising career of usefulness to those who labour in the cause of human improvement, than the islands of New Zealand." It sounded like just the place for a purposeful woman like Mary Taylor.

Even with a wide world to live in, Charlotte stubbornly told her adventurous friend, "I intend to stay." She hung her hope on Monsieur's words, so when he failed to write, she simply had to break the six-months rule and send him a letter. "You showed me once a *little* interest, when I was your pupil in Brussels, and I hold to the maintenance of that *little* interest — I hold to it as I would hold on to life," she wrote. "If my master withdraws his friendship from me entirely I shall be altogether without hope."

Charlotte tried to restore the old closeness she had enjoyed with her teacher, but such desperate words caused Constantin Heger to draw away. At last, hearing nothing to cheer her heart, Charlotte gave up. Wishing no longer to be "the slave of a regret, of a memory; the slave of a fixed and dominant idea which controls the mind," she cut her ties

Mary Taylor sailed to Wellington, New Zealand, which in the 1840s was a small coastal town like this one. Women enjoyed more opportunities in such a young society than they did in England. In 1850 Mary and her cousin Ellen Taylor opened a shop selling draperies, dress fabrics, small toys, and other English goods. Ellen died in 1851, and Mary carried on the business alone.

with the Pensionnat Heger in November 1845. Haworth became her world.

The Reverend Brontë still ministered to the little village, but his vision was failing. He depended on his daughters to read and write for him and to guide him as he walked in the street. The new curate who arrived in 1845 took over many of his pastoral duties. Handsome Arthur

Bell Nicholls, age twenty-seven, came from Ireland. He was the son of a poor farmer, like Patrick Brontë, but after his parents died he was adopted by his uncle, who was headmaster at one of Ireland's best boys' schools. He was more serious and plodding than the charming William Weightman, but the Brontës liked him well enough. "He appears a respectable young man, reads well, and I hope will give satisfaction," Charlotte noted.

When Charlotte said that Nicholls read well, she was referring to the way he read sermons aloud in church. The reading he did for pleasure was a different matter. He preferred dry books on church governance to the kinds of writing the Brontë siblings were producing — fiction and poetry. Branwell, for one, was trying to write a novel. He was blending Angrian legend with his heart's dearest wish to tell the tale of the fictional Maria Thurston. This beautiful married woman falls in love with Alexander Percy, the hero who had fought Satan in one of Branwell's early stories. Charlotte had also started a novel, one that she would call *The Professor*. She drew inspiration from her memories of Brussels. And Anne had begun writing *Agnes Grey*, a novel with a governess as its main character, while still employed at Thorp Green.

Emily was writing something, too, but what? "Many's the time that I have seen Miss Emily put down the 'tally-iron' as she was ironing the clothes to scribble something on a piece of paper," said Martha Brown, who came to the parsonage as a "help-girl," to assist the aging Tabby. "Whatever she was doing, ironing or baking, she had her pencil and paper by her."

One autumn day in 1845, Charlotte happened on a notebook of poems that Emily had written and hidden away. While she was paging through the book, "something more than surprise" took hold of her. Here were verses unlike any she had seen flow from a woman's pen: "They stirred my heart like the sound of a trumpet." These poems brought to Charlotte's ear "a peculiar music — wild, melancholy, and elevating." When she revealed to her remote, self-willed sister that she had read the secret verses, Emily flew into a rage. It took hours for her to quiet down enough to hear Charlotte say how good the poems were.

The angry storm passed, and quiet Anne stepped forward to invite Charlotte to read a stash of poems that *she* had written. Charlotte acknowledged that this poetry was different from Emily's but thought that "these verses too had a sweet sincere pathos of their own."

All three sisters had written poems worthy of being printed in a book — a book that might bring in some money. So on February 6, 1846, a package left Haworth addressed to Aylott and Jones, a small London publishing company. It held the work of three poets with the manly names Currer, Ellis, and Acton Bell.

Women had been publishing novels, poetry, and non-fiction for a century, but whether women should write was controversial. Some Victorian women courageously produced books under their own names. In 1850, for example, Elizabeth Gaskell would take credit for *Mary Barton,* a novel of lower-class life. Other women hid their sex from the reading public by choosing male pseudonyms. One such woman was Mary Ann Evans, who is known to the world as George Eliot, the author of *Middlemarch* and other realistic novels. Evans wanted readers to judge her as a writer rather than as a woman. She wanted to be free to write about any subject, even if people thought it wrong for a female author. For not only did society tell women what they must not do, it also decided which subjects were

The pen name George Eliot gave Mary Ann Evans freedom to write novels that people thought should come from a man.

off limits to them in books and in life. One of these subjects was passion.

Many people agreed with the poet Robert Southey, who had told Charlotte that literature was the business of men. The critic George Henry Lewes asked, "Does it never strike these delightful creatures that their little fingers were meant to be kissed, not to be inked?" In 1854 Lewes and George Eliot would cause a scandal by living together as an unmarried couple. Yet before then Lewes belittled women writers, wondering, "Are there no stockings to darn, no purses to make, no braces [suspenders] to embroider?"

Aylott and Jones agreed to print the Bells' book of poems, and Charlotte, Emily, and Anne managed to come up with the required fee of thirty-one pounds, ten shillings. No one but the sisters knew of their book. Charlotte said nothing about it to Ellen, and she, Emily, and Anne made no mention of it to their father or brother. Emily called Branwell "a hopeless being," and Charlotte remarked, "In his present state it is scarcely possible to stay in the room where he is." She pondered, "What the future has in store — I do not know."

On May 7, 1846, the first copies of *Poems,* by Currer, Ellis, and Acton Bell, reached the Haworth parsonage. The Brontës' book was a slim green volume of sixty-one poems on love, loss, religious faith, and nature. Currer Bell (Charlotte) wrote about risking everything for love in "Passion":

Some have won a wild delight,
*   By daring wilder sorrow;*
Could I gain thy love to-night,
*   I'd hazard death to-morrow.*

In another poem, "Solace," she hinted at a deep emotional
life:

The human heart has hidden treasures,
In secret kept, in silence sealed; —
The thoughts, the hopes, the dreams, the pleasures,
Whose charms were broken if revealed.

Ellis Bell (Emily) proclaimed her kinship with the
night in "Stars":

Oh, stars, and dreams, and gentle night;
*   Oh, night and stars return!*
And hide me from the hostile light,
*   That does not warm, but burn.*

Emily had written "Remembrance" to an imaginary lost
love:

Cold in the earth — and the deep snow piled above thee,
Far, far removed, cold in the dreary grave!

Have I forgot, my only Love, to love thee,
Severed at last by Time's all-severing wave?

Acton Bell (Anne), the most pious of the Brontë sisters, addressed God in the depressing poem "Life":

If life must be so full of care,
Then call me soon to Thee
Or give me strength enough to bear
My load of misery.

It was fortunate for Anne that nature could restore her happiness, as she wrote in "Lines Composed on a Windy Day":

My soul is awakened, my spirit is soaring
And carried aloft on the wings of the breeze;
For above and around me the wild wind is roaring,
Arousing to rapture the earth and the seas.

The three authors barely had the pleasure of holding their finished book in their hands when an emotional crisis threw the Brontë household into turmoil. It began on May 26, when Mr. Edmund Robinson, Anne and Branwell's former employer, died suddenly at age forty-six. Branwell reacted to the news with joy, because the woman he loved was free to marry again. He got ready to join her at Thorp Green as soon as she sent word. The young tutor abruptly learned that he meant less to Lydia Robinson than he had been led to believe, however. Instead of summoning Branwell to her side, she sent her coachman to Haworth with a message. The coachman met Branwell at a local tavern and informed him that he and Mrs. Robinson had no future together.

Branwell had bragged about stealing the older woman's heart, but he loved Mrs. Robinson more than she had ever cared for him. His shock and sorrow were beyond his control. The witnesses who heard his wails compared them to "the bleating of a calf." Lydia Robinson took a further step to prevent Branwell from showing up at Thorp Green unasked. She had her doctor send him a letter stating that his presence would upset her fragile state of mind.

For four nights, Branwell went without sleep. For three days, he ate no food. "To papa he allows rest neither day nor night," Charlotte wrote to Ellen, "and he is continually screwing money out of him sometimes threatening to kill himself if it is withheld from him." According to *Modern Domestic Medicine,* twelve drops of ammonia in a glass of sugared water would calm a drunken man, but Patrick Brontë noted in the margin that this treatment had "only some little effect."

If his family refused to give him money, then Branwell

Jack Shaw the Guardsman, and
Jack painter of Norfolk,

Question — "The half minute time is up, so
Come to the ~~tend~~ scratch; wont you?"
Answer — "Blast your eyes, it's no use, for
I cannot come!"

A PARODY.

Death mocks Branwell Brontë in one of his drawings.

resolved to get it elsewhere. He spent weeks away from home, frequenting the inns and public houses of Halifax, and running up debts.

Meanwhile, the little book called *Poems* received some notice in the press. One reviewer compared it to "a ray of sunshine, gladdening the eye with present glory, and the heart with promise of bright hours in store." This was "good, wholesome, refreshing, vigorous poetry," he proclaimed. Another writer singled out Emily, or "Ellis Bell," for special praise. Here was "a fine quaint spirit" that "may have things to speak that men will be glad to hear, — and an evident power of wing that may reach heights not here attempted."

Yet a single question loomed large in the critics' minds: who were Currer, Ellis, and Acton Bell? Their book offered no clues. Did they live in England or America? Were they alive or dead? One book reviewer rightly guessed, "Perhaps they desired that the poems should be tried and judged upon their own merits alone, apart from all extraneous circumstances."

Even with good reviews and an air of mystery surrounding it, *Poems* failed to find readers. Only two people bought it. Ambitious Charlotte understood that she and her sisters would never support themselves writing poetry. If they were going to make money as writers, they would have to be novelists.

Novels had been growing popular with British readers since the 1700s, when Henry Fielding wrote works like *Tom Jones*, the story of a young man who is turned out of his home and must make his way in the world. *Tom Jones* is a picaresque novel, one that follows the hero's adventures, one after another. Tobias Smollett's humorous *Humphry Clinker*, the tale of a stableman traveling through England with a well-to-do family, is another. Many readers also enjoyed gothic novels, with eerie castles and hints of the supernatural. One of the most famous gothic novels of the early nineteenth century, *Frankenstein,* was written by a woman, Mary Shelley.

As the eighteenth century gave way to the nineteenth, Jane Austen cast a penetrating eye on human nature in *Pride and Prejudice, Emma,* and other novels dealing with families, love, and courtship. Austen influenced the course of fiction by showing authors that they could explore human relationships and depend less on action and thrills. Charlotte Brontë disliked Austen's novels, however. "She does her business of delineating the surface of the lives of genteel English people curiously well," but "the Passions are unknown to her," Charlotte wrote. "Her business is not half so much with the human heart as with the human eyes, mouth, hands and feet."

Victorian novelists strove to present real life on their pages, to observe people's problems and interactions. Some, like George Eliot and Charles Dickens, also cast light on society's ills and the conditions of the lower classes. Dickens published his novels first as serials in magazines. From 1837 to 1839, he brought out *Oliver Twist,* whose title character is one of the many orphans living in London. *Oliver Twist* exposed the harshness of the workhouses that sheltered the poor, the depraved lives of criminals, and the evils of child labor. It also broke new ground by

Many people know Victorian England through the novels of Charles Dickens, who wrote about the prosperous and the poor. This illustration is from his final, unfinished novel, *The Mystery of Edwin Drood.*

presenting a prostitute, the character Nancy, in a sympathetic way. Dickens went on to write other important, socially conscious novels, among them *David Copperfield, Bleak House, Hard Times,* and *Little Dorritt.*

William Makepeace Thackeray, another great Victorian novelist, achieved fame with *Vanity Fair,* which was published first in serial form, in 1847 and 1848. He took a satiric look at society by focusing on two women, the scheming social climber Becky Sharp and her sweet-natured, naïve friend, Amelia Sedley. Thackeray subtitled *Vanity Fair* "A Novel Without a Hero," because every character had flaws.

In July 1846, a second parcel left Haworth addressed to

a London publisher. It held the manuscripts of three novels: *The Professor,* by Currer Bell; *Agnes Grey,* by Acton Bell; and a third by Ellis Bell. Titled *Wuthering Heights,* Emily's novel told a strange, tragic tale of love and revenge on the moors. The sisters hoped their novels would be published together as a three-volume set. But as the three books, as yet unknown, made their way into the world, their authors could only wait for news of them.

In August, despite a throbbing toothache, Charlotte traveled with her father to the city of Manchester, where he was having surgery to restore his sight. The lenses of his eyes had developed cataracts. Removing a lens, if done correctly, would restore the sight in that eye. Patrick Brontë was wide awake throughout the surgery and felt everything, because the doctor performed it without anesthesia. In his copy of *Modern Domestic Medicine,* the Reverend Brontë later noted, "The feeling, under the operation — which lasted fifteen minutes, was of a burning nature — but not intolerable. . . . *My lens* was *extracted* so the cataract can never return in that eye." The doctor removed one lens — the left, because if an infection set in, then only that one eye would be permanently blinded. A month's convalescence in a darkened room followed the surgery. During this time a nurse applied leeches to the patient's temples to reduce inflammation.

Sitting near her father's bed, Charlotte had little to do

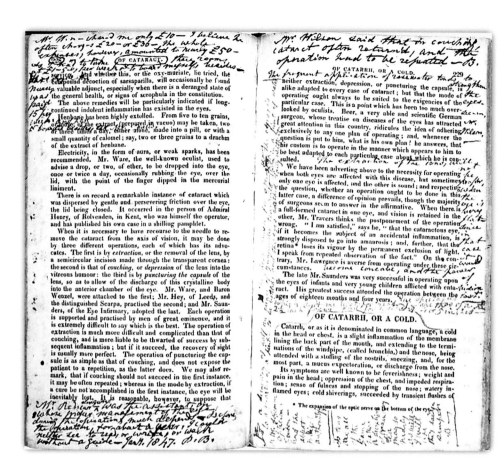

Patrick Brontë's well-used copy of *Modern Domestic Medicine* contained many handwritten notes about ailments that afflicted his family.

except bear with her aching tooth. To pass the time, she began to write another novel. It featured a tiny woman without money and lacking beauty, a person few were likely to notice — "a heroine as small and as plain as myself."

six

"It Is Soul Speaking to Soul"

CHARLOTTE wrote steadily, holding her face close to her pencil and paper, while her father slowly improved. After five days, the doctor removed the Reverend Brontë's bandage. After two weeks, he let the patient sit up. After three weeks, Charlotte dismissed the nurse, whose too-polite servility she distrusted. At the end of the fifth week, she took her father home. Sight returned gradually to Patrick Brontë's left eye; he was writing sermons and reading newspapers without his daughters' help before many more weeks had passed. He felt so confident about resuming his old activities that he sent his curate, Arthur Bell Nicholls, off to Ireland for three weeks, to visit his family.

While the Reverend Brontë healed, his son worsened. Branwell spent most of his time drinking in Halifax and mailing strange letters to his friends. He sent one to the sculptor Joseph Bentley Leyland that read:

Constant and unavoidable depression of mind and body sadly shackle me in even trying to go on with any mental effort which might rescue me from the fate of a dry toast soaked six hours in a glass of cold water, and intended to be given to an old Maid's squeamish Cat.

Branwell's debts piled up. In December 1846, his father and sisters had to settle his accounts to keep him out of jail.

The winter of 1846–47 was discouraging and cold. It was so frigid that Charlotte imagined England had slid north into the Arctic. "The sky looks like ice — the earth is frozen, the wind is as keen as a two-edged blade," she wrote to Ellen Nussey. Everyone in the parsonage caught colds. Anne's developed into asthma, and Patrick Brontë came down with influenza. In the village below, rising prices for bread and potatoes forced many weavers' families to do without. Hunger, dangerous conditions in textile mills, and contaminated water led to poorer health and climbing death rates.

Through the winter and spring, one publishing house after another rejected the sisters' novels. Then, at last, in

July 1847, a year after they first posted their manuscripts, the publisher T. C. Newby agreed to print *Agnes Grey* and *Wuthering Heights* as a three-volume set, if the authors put up fifty pounds. (*Wuthering Heights* would take up two volumes, and *Agnes Grey* would fill a third.) Anne and Emily would get their money back when — and if — their novels earned a big enough profit. Whether T. C. Newby rejected *The Professor* or its author refused to pay for publication is unknown. But Charlotte continued to send out her novel every time it came back, crossing out one publisher's address on the wrapping and scribbling in a new one.

The seventh firm to receive the manuscript responded with a long letter. Smith, Elder and Company was rejecting *The Professor,* like all the others, but the gentlemen wondered if Currer Bell had a longer work to submit. If so, they promised to give it close attention. Publishers preferred longer novels that could be printed in three-volume sets, as a book that could be purchased in installments was easy for many readers to afford. Also, the circulating libraries that served cities and towns liked the three-volume system because three patrons could read one novel at the same time.

It just so happened that Currer Bell had a longer novel. Charlotte spent the next month finishing the book with the small, plain heroine. She packaged it and mailed it to Smith, Elder and Company, 65, Cornhill, London. Its title was *Jane Eyre.*

George Smith, who managed the company, started reading Currer Bell's book on a Sunday. Smith was twenty-three and had taken over Smith, Elder and Company in 1846, after his father died. The novel intrigued him so much that he canceled plans to go horseback riding. He gulped down his dinner so he could return to Jane Eyre's story, and he stayed up late that night, unwilling to sleep until he had read every word. The next day, Smith wrote to Currer Bell again, to offer one hundred pounds for the right to publish *Jane Eyre*. If the novel proved popular enough to be reprinted or published in other countries, then Currer Bell might earn as much as five hundred pounds.

Charlotte Brontë understood that she could never support herself for life on a hundred pounds, but it thrilled her to know that a publisher had spotted her talent. She agreed to the terms that Smith offered, but she put her

Just twenty-four years old when Charlotte Brontë first sent him her work, George Smith would become the foremost publisher in Victorian England. As an older man he recalled his friendships with Brontë and other great writers as "the happiest and most characteristic feature of my business life."

foot down when he asked her to rewrite parts of her book. Some scenes in *Jane Eyre* were too brutal, Smith thought.

The author explained that while writing she had immersed herself in the spirit of the work. She had lived every sorrow and joy along with her main character. "Were I to retrench, to alter and add now when I am uninterested and cold," she wrote, "I know I should only further injure what may be already defective." She urged Smith to have confidence in his fellow Victorians. *Jane Eyre* "might suit the public taste better than you anticipate — for it is true and Truth has a severe charm of its own," she stated.

On October 19, 1847, *Jane Eyre: An Autobiography* ("Edited by Currer Bell") became the first novel by a Brontë to be published. Its pages introduced the world to a new kind of female character. Society easily overlooked women like Jane Eyre, drably dressed and lacking beauty and wealth. Yet as they followed Jane from childhood to maturity, readers found her to be a person of deep feeling and the equal of any man. Outspoken and courageous, she stood in contrast to the passive woman who was the Victorian ideal.

"There was no possibility of taking a walk that day." A cold winter wind blows around the great house called Gateshead as *Jane Eyre* begins. Clouds block the sky, and a heavy rain hammers the ground. The bleakness outdoors matches the leaden mood within, where the orphaned

Jane has taken refuge with a book. She tries to distract herself with its pictures, but even these are dreary: a lone rock emerging from the sea, a headstone in a moonlit graveyard, a demon besetting a thief.

Ten-year-old Jane is an unwanted child. Her widowed aunt, Mrs. Reed, resents being saddled with her care and treats her harshly. Jane is just a little girl, but she stands up for herself and for the truth. She speaks out when she is punished unfairly, in a way that bothers her aunt's conscience: "My Uncle Reed is in heaven, and can see all you do and think; and so can papa and mamma; they know how you shut me up all day long, and how you wish me dead." Mrs. Reed solves the problem of this "passionate" child by sending her away to school.

Jane will spend the next nine years at Lowood Institution, as both pupil and teacher. In describing Lowood, Charlotte Brontë brought to life the Clergy Daughters' School. The Reverend Mr. Brocklehurst, the headmaster, is another William Carus Wilson, "a black pillar" of a man with a grim face "like a carved mask." Brocklehurst uses religion to justify mistreating the girls. "When you put bread and cheese, instead of burnt porridge, into these children's mouths, you may indeed feed their vile bodies," he says, "but you little think how you starve their immortal souls!"

Jane befriends a fellow pupil, Helen Burns, who is a bright girl and a good student. Like the oldest Brontë sister,

THE WINTER GULL.

WINTER MEW, OR CODDY MODDY.

(Larus hybernus, Lin.—La Mouette d'hyver, Buff.)

THIS generally exceeds the Common Gull in its weight
and admeasurement. The bill is lightish, except at the
tip, of a slender shape, and about two inches long: irides
hazel. It is marked with oblong dusky spots on the top
of the head and hinder part of the neck: back and sca-
pulars pale ash-coloured grey; but these feathers are
spotted with brown: wing coverts pale brown, edged
with dingy white; the first quill is black, the six following more or less black at the ends; the others tipped
with white: the tail is crossed with a broad black bar
near the end: all the other parts of the plumage are
white: legs bluish dirty white. Mr Pennant asserts that
this is only a young bird, not a species distinct from the
Common Gull; and he also differs from Linnæus in his
opinion that it is the same as the *Larus tridactylus*, or
Tarrock.

Young Jane Eyre was reading *A History of British Birds,* a book the
Brontës owned that had peculiar illustrations. On one page a rock
stands alone, battered by a winter sea. It symbolizes Jane's isolation.

Maria, Helen suffers constant abuse from a cruel teacher, whom Charlotte gave an ugly name, Miss Scatcherd.

Miss Scatcherd even interrupts a history lesson to shout at Helen, "You dirty, disagreeable girl! you have never cleaned your nails this morning!" For this crime against cleanliness, Miss Scatcherd gives Helen a flogging. Helen accepts punishment without complaining as Jane, like Charlotte as a child, looks on powerlessly. "Love your enemies," Helen quotes from the Bible to Jane; "bless them that curse you; do good to them that hate you and despite-

Wrongly labeled a liar, Jane Eyre is forced to stand before the rest of Lowood School, humiliated. Peggy Ann Garner played young Jane in the 1944 film version of Charlotte Brontë's first novel.

fully use you." Jane rejects such a passive faith, declaring, "I was no Helen Burns."

Charlotte Brontë insisted that the brutality she described was real. What was more, the treatment Maria endured at school was worse than anything Helen Burns had to suffer. Some of it was so savage it defied belief. "I abstained from recording much that I remembered respecting her, lest the narrative should sound incredible," Charlotte wrote, recalling Maria.

With friends like Helen and a kind teacher, Miss Temple, Jane survives her years at Lowood and even flourishes. Once she has grown up, the desire to live in the wider world impels her to leave the school. She journeys to an estate called Thornfield Hall, to be governess to a young girl named Adèle Varens. Adèle has spent most of her life in France and speaks little English.

Even at Thornfield Hall, Jane longs for more. She tells her readers that "women feel just as men feel; they need exercise for their faculties, and a field for their efforts as much as their brothers do; they suffer from too rigid a restraint, too absolute a stagnation, precisely as men suffer."

In *Jane Eyre*, Charlotte Brontë showed the awkward invisibility of a governess's life. When well-to-do guests stay at Thornfield, Jane must sit alone in a shaded nook off the drawing room. Her gray dress contrasts with the silks and jewels of the fine ladies who discuss her openly, as if she lacks a mind and feelings. Jane's employer sees her worth, however, and seeks her friendship. He is Edward Rochester, master of Thornfield. Rochester is a dark, brooding man, who describes himself as "heart-weary and soul-withered." Adèle is his ward. Rochester lets down his guard in Jane's steady, intelligent presence. She learns to recognize his approach by the "warning fragrance" of his cigar. Rochester mentions his past mistakes but advises her not to grow too curious about him. "Don't long for poison," he cautions. "Encroach, presume, and the game is up." Jane understands that he — and his house — harbor secrets. Strange things happen, and she cannot help but wonder: Who set fire to Rochester's bed, perhaps trying to kill him? What is the source of the "demoniac laugh" that rings out in the night?

Edward Rochester is older than Jane Eyre and worldly, yet he and the governess fall in love. As the two agree to marry, a violent storm erupts. Lightning strikes an old chestnut tree in Thornfield's garden, leaving it split and broken, like the one near Ellen Nussey's home. This is an ominous sign, and as the wedding is about to take place, Rochester's dreadful secret is revealed. Jane learns that she cannot be Rochester's wife.

Refusing to be his mistress, Jane runs away. She finds a measure of contentment teaching in a school, but another man has a purpose for her in mind. He is bound for India

Jane Eyre and Edward Rochester, portrayed by Mia Wasikowska and Michael Fassbender, find love in the 2011 motion picture *Jane Eyre*.

as a missionary and wants her to go with him as his wife. He makes no promise of love; instead he wants Jane to be his partner in work. She is close to surrendering when her heart hears Rochester crying out for her, as clearly as if his voice were traveling across the miles. She goes to him, to discover his fate and her own.

The published book thrilled its first readers. Among them was the novelist William Makepeace Thackeray, who almost wished that he had never read *Jane Eyre:* "It interested me so much that I have lost (or won if you like) a whole day in reading it at the busiest period." Thackeray admitted, "Some of the love passages made me cry."

The critic George Henry Lewes was quick to recognize

THE LUNATIC SPRANG AND GRAPPLED
HIS THROAT VICIOUSLY

Edward Rochester reveals to Jane Eyre the shocking secret of
Thornfield Hall on what would have been their wedding day.
This illustration is from a 1922 edition of *Jane Eyre*.

the greatness of *Jane Eyre*. "It is soul speaking to soul," he
wrote excitedly; "it is an utterance from the depths of a
struggling, suffering, much-enduring spirit." He found in
it "perception of character and power of delineating it; pic-
turesqueness; passion; and knowledge of life." Lewes noted

that *Jane Eyre* is one of those rare novels that stay with the reader once the final words have been read. This is because "reality — deep, significant reality — is the great characteristic of the book."

"The writer is evidently a woman," he decided. Lewes could make fun of women novelists, but *Jane Eyre* was so good that he was willing to overlook Currer Bell's sex. "Man or woman, young or old, be that as it may," he wrote, because "no such book has gladdened our eyes for a long while."

Another critic called *Jane Eyre* "a novel of remarkable power and beauty." He believed that "many of the scenes through which the author has passed, as well as the feelings which she describes, are real." This reviewer, too, guessed that Bell was a woman. He praised the main character, Jane Eyre, stating that she "is drawn by one whose pen is cunning to describe every nook and turning in the female heart." He found the descriptions of Rochester less than perfect, though. This was no surprise, given his view that "a female pen is inadequate to pourtray the character and the passions of a man."

People were clamoring to read Currer Bell's novel. Smith, Elder and Company published a second edition in England, which Charlotte dedicated to Thackeray, and then a third and a fourth. In January 1848, the first American edition appeared. Soon, people in the towns around Haworth were starting to read *Jane Eyre*. Charlotte even

Praise from the influential critic George Henry Lewes brought many readers to Currer Bell's novel. The book's greatness made the author's sex unimportant, Lewes wrote.

overheard a local clergyman remark on elements in the book that seemed familiar: "Why, they have got Cowan Bridge School, and Mr Carus Wilson here, I declare!"

"He did not recognize Currer Bell," Charlotte noted in a letter to Smith, Elder and Company. Clearly, she enjoyed her secret. "What author would be without the advantage of being able to walk invisible?" she asked. She kept the news of her authorship from Ellen Nussey, who might have disapproved, but she sent *Jane Eyre* to Mary Taylor in New Zealand. It surprised Mary to discover that her friend had created a novel that was "so perfect as a work of art." Socially conscious Mary wanted to know how Charlotte could write a whole book without once preaching to her readers about society's wrongs.

Emily and Anne convinced Charlotte that the time had come to tell their father about her novel. Charlotte chose a morning when he was reading in his study to knock on his door and say, "Papa, I have been writing a book." He looked up to scold, "I hope you have not been involving yourself in any such silly expense." Charlotte replied to the contrary: "I think I shall gain some money by it." She read him some reviews and left him with a copy of *Jane Eyre.*

Patrick Brontë almost always ate alone, but that afternoon he asked his daughters to join him for tea. When they were seated, he announced, "Children, Charlotte has been writing a book — and I think it is a better one than I expected."

Charlotte Brontë had taken the art of fiction to a new level. She had written frankly about a woman's feelings at a depth no other writer had yet explored. Her frankness bothered some readers, and after the first flurry of praise, unfriendly reviews began to appear. "In 'Jane Eyre' the immorality is peculiar"; "Religion is stabbed in the dark — our social distinctions attempted to be leveled, and all absurdly moral notions done away with"; "It would be no credit to any one to be the author of 'Jane Eyre.'"

The angriest criticism came from a woman named Elizabeth Rigby, who condemned the main character, Jane Eyre, as "the personification of an unregenerate and undisciplined spirit." Jane's moral strength "is the strength of a mere heathen mind which is a law unto itself," she wrote. The entire novel was "an anti-Christian composition." And even though she recognized the high quality of Brontë's writing, she dismissed the novel as a failure.

Rigby decided that Currer Bell had to be a man, "for if we ascribe the book to a woman at all, we have no alternative but to ascribe it to one who has, for some sufficient reason, long forfeited the society of her own sex." She could not resist adding that "if by no woman, it is certainly also by no artist." This review made Charlotte Brontë furious. She kept it — and others like it — from her father, but she responded to their authors in the preface to the second edition of *Jane Eyre.* She reminded those "in whose eyes whatever is unusual is wrong" that "conventionality is not morality."

This might have been true, but *Jane Eyre* was becoming a dangerous book, one that decent mothers forbade their daughters to read. What caused this shift in public opinion? Could it have been the appearance of another novel, an even more disturbing one, written by a different Bell? Some readers struggled with *Jane Eyre.* But hardly anyone knew what to make of *Wuthering Heights.*

"Moorish, and Wild, and Knotty as a Root of Heath"

W HEN the air was in an uproar and rainy squalls blew over the Yorkshire moors, the locals had a word for it: *wuthering.* Emily Brontë grew up hearing this word from Tabby Aykroyd and other country folk, and in 1846, she wrote it down. Emily gave the name *Wuthering Heights* to her only novel and to a home that is central to the story it tells. It is there that Emily's dark tale of destructive love, cruelty, and early death begins.

Just a few stunted firs and thorn bushes grow near Wuthering Heights, a farmhouse on a lonely, windswept moor, miles from any neighbors. Strange things happen there. Ghostly fingers tap at its windows; a tortured man lives within its walls and brings those around him to ruin.

But these dreadful goings-on have yet to happen when Catherine Earnshaw's father returns from Liverpool with a mysterious child, a boy who is dirty and ragged and "dark almost as if it came from the devil." Mr. Earnshaw christens the child Heathcliff and intends to raise him as his own. Young Catherine and Heathcliff form a kinship that is stronger than any blood tie. They become inseparable friends, a rebellious pair who like nothing better than to run freely on the moors. Meanwhile, Mr. Earnshaw's love for the boy consumes Catherine's older brother, Hindley,

Laurence Olivier was Heathcliff and Merle Oberon played Catherine in the 1939 film *Wuthering Heights.*

with deadly envy. After years pass, Mr. Earnshaw dies, and Hindley marries and becomes the master of Wuthering Heights. Hindley takes revenge on Heathcliff by forcing him to labor on the farm, but the bond between Heathcliff and Catherine stays as strong as ever, even as they grow up and life draws them apart.

At Wuthering Heights, emotions like jealousy and love are forces as wild and savage as the harshest weather. But another moorland house, Thrushcross Grange, is a place of comfort and refinement. There, the Linton family enjoys a peaceful, genteel life supported by wealth. Their fine clothes and manners attract Catherine, and when kind, docile Edgar Linton asks her to marry him, she accepts.

Her choice sets off a dark sequence of revenge and destruction that leaves no one unhurt. Heathcliff hardens into a sinister Byronic figure whose heart is closed to everyone but Catherine. He acquires wealth and wins possession of Wuthering Heights and, later, Thrushcross Grange. He elopes with Edgar Linton's sister, Isabella, only to cause pain. Isabella will ask what many readers have pondered: Is Heathcliff a man or a devil?

As for Catherine, she will shock Victorian readers by claiming that she has no place in heaven; her soul belongs on the moors. "I'm wearying to escape into that glorious world, and to be always there; not seeing it dimly through tears, and yearning for it through the walls of an aching heart; but really with it, and in it." Rejecting earthly existence, Catherine retreats to her room, where she refuses food and steadily weakens. She and Heathcliff meet for the last time in her bedchamber on a Sunday, while Edgar is at church and Catherine lies close to death. They kiss and embrace, yet each blames and accuses the other. "You have killed me — and thriven on it, I think. How strong you are!" cries Catherine, who is beautiful in her frailty.

"You have killed yourself," Heathcliff argues back. "I have not broken your heart — *you* have broken it — and in breaking it, you have broken mine." Catherine sinks into unconsciousness, and she dies that night after giving birth prematurely to a daughter, another Catherine, or Cathy.

So much has happened, but Emily Brontë has told only half her story. In the second part of her novel, it will be the task of another generation to restore joy and hope to Wuthering Heights.

Emily Brontë devised a complex structure for *Wuthering Heights.* She told her tale through the diary of a character named Lockwood, who some years later is a new tenant at Thrushcross Grange. When he rides up to Wuthering Heights on a winter day to call on his landlord, Mr. Heathcliff, a snowstorm forces him to spend the night. A servant shows him to a chamber that was never used, explaining that the master rarely allowed it to be entered. As Lock-

SHE REMAINED, CALLING AT INTERVALS,
AND THEN LISTENING

Catherine calls into a storm for Heathcliff in this early illustration.

wood drifts into sleep, half dreaming, he hears a tree blowing against the window beside his bed. The window refuses to open, so he breaks a pane of glass and reaches out to snap off the bothersome branch. To his surprise, he grasps not twigs, but tiny, cold fingers. His cries bring Heathcliff into the room. By this time the spirit has gone, but what

Lockwood sees next is equally shocking. His landlord throws open the window and in anguish begs his beloved Cathy to enter.

Lockwood goes home to Thrushcross Grange, and as often happens to people in nineteenth-century novels, exposure to wintry air gives him a bad cold. While he rests in bed, his housekeeper tells him the saga of Wuthering Heights. In this way, Emily Brontë's novel becomes a tale within a tale, as Lockwood records in his diary the housekeeper's story.

Wuthering Heights belongs to the Yorkshire landscape, Charlotte Brontë said. "It is moorish, and wild, and knotty as a root of heath. Nor was it natural that it should be otherwise; the author being herself a native and nursling of the moors."

But was there anything natural about *Wuthering Heights*? "The characters are as false as they are loathsome," one outraged critic declared. He pronounced Heathcliff, Hindley, Catherine, and the rest "a perfect pandemonium of low and brutal creatures, who wrangle with each other in language too disgusting for the eye or the ear to tolerate." This critic had no idea how Ellis Bell's novel ended, because after reading a few offending scenes, he "took the liberty of declining the honour of a farther acquaintance."

Ellis Bell's skill as a writer failed to excuse the "strange wild pictures" that he had created, another reviewer wrote.

Rather, Bell's powerful talent succeeded only in "heightening their repulsiveness." The editors of a weekly newspaper promised their readers "that they have never read anything like it before." *Wuthering Heights* was so puzzling

I SOUGHT, AND SOON DISCOVERED, THE
THREE HEAD-STONES

Lockwood stands at the graves of Edgar, Catherine, and Heathcliff and wonders "how anyone could ever imagine unquiet slumbers, for the sleepers in that quiet earth."

that the editors concluded, "We must leave it to our readers to decide what sort of book it is."

Today people might decide that the behavior Emily Brontë described was dysfunctional. Harmful relationships are nothing new, though; human beings have hurt one another through their words and actions in every period of history. But to the prim Victorians, this side of life was to be kept hidden. It was to be ignored, if possible, and certainly not displayed in a novel for anyone to read. Emily cut out some reviews and saved them in her desk drawer, but neither she nor Anne ever told their father that they were published authors.

While the two-volume *Wuthering Heights* was causing so much noisy comment, the third volume in the set, *Agnes Grey,* slipped quietly into the world. To the relief of the few critics who bothered to notice it, Acton Bell's slender novel offered a clear moral lesson: it taught readers "to put every trust in a supreme wisdom and goodness." This was the author's intention. "Such humble talents as God has given me I will endeavour to put to their greatest use," Anne stated. "If I am able to amuse, I will try to benefit too; and when I feel it my duty to speak an unpalatable truth, with the help of God, I will speak it." This is why her novel began with the words, "All true histories contain instruction."

Yet this author, like the other Bells, chose "subjects that

are peculiar without being either probable or pleasing," some critics lamented. It hardly mattered that *Agnes Grey* was written well; "the injudicious selection of the theme and matter" marred the work. Anne's tale contained no dark secret or deadly revenge. Instead, its tyranny and cruelty were truer to life. Anne had described everyday behavior in well-to-do households.

Emily Brontë found the raw material for *Wuthering Heights* in her imagination, but Anne drew on her own experience, as Charlotte had done. Her main character, Agnes Grey, comes from a poor but respectable clergyman's family, and she seeks a post as a governess, like Jane Eyre. Recounting Agnes's adventures among the families that employ her, Anne revealed much that she had seen and done as governess to the Inghams and Robinsons. Her account sounded so true to life that one reviewer supposed Acton Bell — this man — "must have bribed some governess very largely, either with love or money, to reveal to him the secrets of her prison-house."

Also like Jane Eyre, Agnes tells her own story. "How delightful it would be to be a governess! To go out into the world; to enter upon a new life; to act for myself," Agnes thinks. She wants, too, "to earn my own maintenance, and something to comfort and help my father, mother, and sister." She finds the governess's life anything but delightful when she is given charge of three impossible children in the Bloomfield family. Seven-year-old Tom, "the flower of the flock — a generous, noble-spirited boy," according to his mother, delights in cutting up live birds with his pen-knife. It shocks Agnes that Tom's father and uncle encourage this gruesome hobby. Tom and his sisters refuse to obey Agnes, knowing their parents have forbidden her to punish them, while the parents blame Miss Grey for the children's tantrums and wild behavior. A frustrated Agnes pulls six-year-old Mary Ann's hair and shakes her violently in a desperate effort to make her cooperate. But these methods of discipline, questionable at best, do no good. The Bloomfields fire Miss Grey before a year has passed.

Agnes likes life somewhat better with the second family to employ her, the Murrays of Horton Lodge. Her new pupils include two teenage girls, Rosalie and Matilda. Rosalie is sixteen and pretty, but she thinks only of the impression she makes and the hearts she can conquer. Fourteen-year-old Matilda is a big, active girl who uses rough language and feels most at home in the stable. Mrs. Murray orders the governess to "oblige, instruct, refine, and polish" these girls, or, as Agnes observes, to "render them as superficially attractive and showily accomplished as they could possibly be made." Securing wealthy husbands is to be their great aim in life.

After her father's death, Agnes returns home to help her mother run a school. She feels some regret at leaving Rosa-

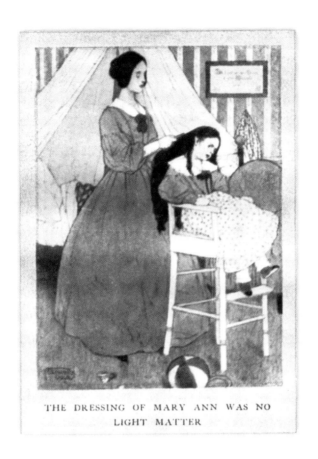

THE DRESSING OF MARY ANN WAS NO
LIGHT MATTER

Agnes Grey struggles with Mary Ann's hair in this 1922 illustration.

lie, who has grown close to her, and a new curate, Edward
Weston, of whom she is fond. A year later, Agnes returns
to the neighborhood of Horton Lodge to visit Rosalie, who
is married to the wealthy Sir Thomas Ashby. Rosalie has
done what was expected of her. She has a grand home and
a baby, but she detests her husband and her life with him.
"And as for all the wisdom and goodness you have been
trying to instil into me — that is all very right and proper

I dare say, and if I were some twenty years older, I might fructify by it," she admits to Agnes Grey. "But people must enjoy themselves when they are young!"

Agnes tells her readers, "Of course, I pitied her exceedingly, as well for her false idea of happiness and disregard of duty, as for the wretched partner with whom her fate was linked." In contrast to Rosalie, Agnes earns the love of pious Mr. Weston and the happiness she deserves through virtue and bending of inclination to duty.

The publisher of these two novels, T. C. Newby, turned out to care only about making a quick profit. Thanks to sloppy editing, his editions of *Wuthering Heights* and *Agnes Grey* contained many punctuation errors and misspellings. Even Agnes Grey's name appeared as "Anges" on several pages. Much later it would come to light that he lied to the sisters about how many books he had printed and sold so he could cheat them out of money they had earned. In 1854, Charlotte, as the last surviving sister, would receive ninety pounds that should have been paid to Emily and Anne.

While Charlotte, Emily, and Anne continued writing, they also did the duties expected of a minister's unmarried daughters. One of these was to sit and visit with ladies who called at the parsonage. One day, they spent two hours listening to a woman named Mrs. Collins, who told a tale of triumph over woe.

Six years earlier, this good woman had lived with her husband in Keighley. Mr. Collins had been a curate, a man of the cloth, but in his drunkenness he used to beat his wife and children. His reckless spending plunged the couple into debt, and finally his bad habits led to his dismissal. Mr. Collins abandoned his ailing wife and their offspring in Manchester and took off for places unknown. Slowly, Mrs. Collins worked to restore her health and reputation. When she called in Haworth she could boast that she was an independent woman who ran a lodging house in Manchester, and that she had saved her children from their father's violence and bad example.

Anne soaked up every word.

eight

"A Dreadful Darkness Closes In"

THE public's great interest in *Jane Eyre* brought invitations through her publisher to venture into society, but Charlotte turned them down. In February 1848, a London theater company presented a play based on her novel, but she declined to see it. Stepping out meant telling the world that Currer Bell was really Charlotte Brontë of Haworth. Charlotte preferred to keep her secret, to stay home and write with her sisters. In the evening, after their father had retired to his bedchamber, they read aloud to one another from their work in progress.

While Charlotte searched her imagination for the story of her next book, Anne finished a second novel, *The Ten-*

ant of Wildfell Hall. Anne stubbornly had it published by T. C. Newby, despite his slipshod handling of *Agnes Grey,* but she soon regretted her decision. Hoping to make a big profit on an American edition, the shady publisher told a U.S. firm that Anne's new book was written by the author of the best-selling *Jane Eyre.* In other words, Currer and Acton Bell were really the same person. Word got around, and soon Charlotte received a perplexed letter from George Smith of Smith, Elder and Company. He demanded an explanation, and he deserved one, because Currer Bell's next novel had been promised to him.

The sisters knew that the time had come to reveal their separate identities — at least to their publishers. So in July 1848, Charlotte and Anne packed a small box. One day after tea, they walked four miles through a thunderstorm to Keighley, where they boarded a train to the West Yorkshire city of Leeds. There they caught an overnight train to London. Emily, the most private and homebound of the three, had flatly refused to go.

Anne and Charlotte reached the great city at eight in the morning and went to their lodging, the Chapter Coffee House. It was an old, paneled place where gentlemen stayed. It was thought unsuitable for ladies on their own, but the Brontë sisters came from the country and knew no better. They washed up, had breakfast, and set out on their errand.

London was "the Emporium of the World," noted a writer in 1847. It was a place of "magnificent squares, and noble mansions, —tenanted by persons of the highest rank." Such a view ignored the poverty that Dickens and others described.

That morning, George Smith was hard at work at his desk, with a busy day ahead of him. He was less than pleased to hear that two ladies had come to see him, and that they declined to give their names. Smith had them shown into his office and vowed to deal quickly with this irksome interruption. He looked up to see two "rather quaintly dressed little ladies, pale-faced and anxious-looking." The smaller one handed him a letter that he had written to Currer Bell.

Smith glanced at the letter in his hand, and then at the woman. He looked again at the letter, and back at the woman. Several moments passed before he understood that he was meeting the author of *Jane Eyre*. His morning's work forgotten, he introduced the Misses Brontë to his colleague William Smith Williams, a gentle older man. His earlier annoyance transformed into joy, George Smith suddenly wanted the Brontës to see London's sights and its people. He urged them to view the latest art exhibition. He talked excitedly of presenting them to his mother and sisters, and to Thackeray and Lewes.

No, Charlotte said, although she would have loved to meet these literary stars. She and Anne were telling their secret to their publishers alone. The rest of the world must go on thinking of the Bells as three gentlemen, she insisted. But wouldn't they at least attend a party while pretending to be his "country cousins," Smith asked. Charlotte saw that "he would have liked some excitement," but again she said no.

That evening, Smith called for Charlotte and Anne at their hotel. He was with his two sisters and William Smith Williams, and all were elegantly dressed. They were on their way to the opera and insisted the Brontës come along. Charlotte's head ached, and she and Anne had nothing fancy to wear, but they put on their best country dresses and went anyway. "Fine ladies and gentlemen glanced at us with a slight, graceful superciliousness quite warranted by the circumstances — still I felt pleasurably excited," Charlotte reported to Mary Taylor, "and I saw Anne was calm and gentle which she always is."

Charlotte Brontë and George Smith later wrote down their impressions of each other. In a letter to Mary Taylor, Charlotte summed up Smith as "a firm, intelligent man of business though so young." He was "bent on getting on — and I think desirous to make his way by fair, honourable means." Smith was "enterprising — but likewise cool & cautious." And, finally, "Mr. Smith is a practical man."

Long after Charlotte Brontë's death, George Smith confessed that he thought she looked "interesting rather

A plaque at 65, Cornhill, London, commemorates the visit of Charlotte and Anne Brontë to Smith, Elder and Company.

than attractive. She was very small, and had a quaint old-fashioned look. Her head seemed too large for her body. She had fine eyes, but her face was marred by the shape of the mouth." Charlotte displayed very little "feminine charm," and, Smith perceived, "of this fact she herself was uneasily and perpetually conscious. It may seem strange that the possession of genius did not lift her above the weakness of an excessive anxiety about her personal appearance. But I believe she would have given all her genius and her fame to have been beautiful."

Anne Brontë, wrote Smith, "was a gentle, quiet, rather subdued person, by no means pretty, yet of a pleasing appearance. Her manner was curiously expressive of a wish for protection and encouragement, a kind of constant appeal which invited sympathy." Anne proved that appearances can deceive, because her new book was not only frank, but downright shocking.

The Tenant of Wildfell Hall begins in the village of Linden-Car, where everyone seems curious about Helen Graham, the woman who has come to live in the old stone mansion called Wildfell Hall. Helen is the mother of a five-year-old boy, and apparently she is a widow, but she remains aloof from village society. Her dark beauty entrances a young farmer named Gilbert Markham, yet Helen resists growing close to him. When Gilbert presses her to know why, she gives him her diary to read. This diary reveals Helen's secret — that her real name is Helen Huntingdon, and her husband lives.

Helen has written in the diary about her life before marriage and her attraction to handsome Arthur Huntingdon. She was determined to marry Arthur despite her aunt's warning that he was "destitute of principle, and prone to every vice that is common to youth." Helen believed that he would mend his ways if she set a good example, but she discovered her mistake too late, after she and Arthur were married.

Anne Brontë shied away from nothing when describing Arthur Huntingdon's nights of drinking with his wild, wasted friends. "There are scenes in which the author seems to pride himself in bringing his reader into the closest possible proximity with naked vice," one critic wrote about Acton Bell's novel, "and there are conversations such as we had hoped never to see printed in English." These scenes shock few readers today, but no novelist before Anne Brontë had described drunken behavior in such a straightforward, realistic way:

> *Mr. Hattersley burst into the room with a clamorous volley of oaths in his mouth. . . . Arthur placed himself beside poor Milicent [Helen's friend], confidentially pushing his head into her face, and drawing in closer to*

her as she shrunk away from him. He was not so noisy as Hattersley, but his face was exceedingly flushed, he laughed incessantly, and while I blushed for all I saw and heard of him, I was glad that he chose to talk to his companion in so low a tone that no one could hear what he said but herself.

When he was not drinking, Arthur amused himself by telling Helen about his past loves and bringing her to tears. At last he aroused her anger and provoked her to say that if he had told her these stories sooner, she never would have married him. When Arthur laughed and claimed to know Helen better than she knew herself, she responded with action rather than with words. "Without another word I left the room and locked myself up in my own chamber," she wrote in her diary. Arthur begged to come in, but Helen kept the door locked until morning.

This was another scene that made readers gasp, because it was the rare Victorian wife who would have denied her husband entry into her bed. To do so was a bold statement of female independence. "The slamming of that bedroom door fairly resounds through the long emptiness of Anne's novel," commented a writer of a later generation, May Sinclair.

Helen endured her unhappy marriage until Arthur started luring their little son into his habits, giving the

WITH A SUDDEN EFFORT SHE WITHDREW
HER HAND

Helen Graham's resistance to his friendship puzzles Gilbert
Markham in Anne Brontë's novel *The Tenant of Wildfell Hall.*

child wine in order to "make a man of him." Helen tried
keeping little Arthur in the nursery while the men were
drinking, but when his father wanted the boy with him,
she had to comply. Husbands had custody of the children
in a marriage, just as they took possession of their wives'
property. The words of Sir William Blackstone, an eighteenth-century legal scholar, were still true in Victorian

England: "In law, the husband and wife are one person and the husband is that person."

To protect her son, Helen left. A divorce was out of the question. She had no right to one, and even if she did, she had no money to pay for it. Besides, in a divorce Arthur would take their child. Her only option was to run away, and in doing so break the law. She turned for help to her brother, who helped her settle at Wildfell Hall. There she supported herself and her son by painting, using an assumed name. Like Mrs. Collins, the curate's wife who visited Haworth parsonage, Helen lived independently and protected her son from his father's bad habits.

The diary ends at this point, but the story continues. Helen learns that Arthur Huntingdon is gravely ill, and she goes home to nurse him. She can do little for this sick man as he lies in pain and torment, unable to repent. "What is God—I cannot see Him or hear Him?" Arthur asks. "God is only an idea," he says. To deny faith was to make a bold admission in the Victorian period. From a religious writer like Anne Brontë, this was a statement of despair. Arthur dies a tortured soul. A year passes before Gilbert Markham, the farmer, seeks Helen Huntingdon to learn if he has a future with her.

Because it was by Anne Brontë, *The Tenant of Wildfell Hall* taught moral lessons. It warned against choosing a mate for looks rather than character, and it showed clearly what happens to people who give themselves up to drinking. Nevertheless, its unblinking scenes of vice were what caught people's attention. "There seems in the writer a morbid love for the coarse, not to say the brutal," remarked one reviewer. "There is a coarseness of tone throughout the writing of all these Bells, that puts an offensive subject in its worst point of view."

The comments hurt, but Anne defended her book by taking aim at a society that covered up anything it wished not to see. "If there were less of this delicate concealment of facts — this whispering 'Peace, peace,' when there is no peace, there would be less of sin and misery," she wrote in the preface to the second edition of *The Tenant of Wildfell Hall.* She assured her readers that men like Arthur Huntingdon did indeed exist. "If I have warned one rash youth from following in their steps," she wrote, "or prevented one thoughtless girl from falling into the very natural error of my heroine, the book has not been written in vain."

She knew that men like Huntingdon existed, because she had one for a brother. Patrick Brontë tried to limit his son's drinking and drug use by locking Branwell up with him in his bedchamber at night, but the hours of forced sobriety brought on the condition known as delirium tremens, which is characterized by shaking, confusion, and hallucinations. Charlotte confided to Ellen Nussey, "Papa — and sometimes all of us have sad nights with him."

In September 1848, Francis Grundy went to Haworth to see his old friend from the Luddendenfoot railroad station. He took a room at the local inn, ordered dinner for two, and sent word to the parsonage for Branwell to join him. When he answered a knock at his door, though, he let in not Branwell, but Branwell's father. "He spoke of Branwell with more affection than I had ever heretofore heard him express," Grundy wrote, "but he also spoke almost hopelessly." The Reverend Brontë warned that Branwell had been ill in bed, but said that he would be coming shortly.

Patrick Brontë departed, and soon Grundy saw Branwell peering around the edge of the door. His head "was a mass of red, unkempt, uncut hair, wildly floating round a great, gaunt forehead; the cheeks yellow and hollow, the mouth fallen, the thin white lips not trembling but shaking, the sunken eyes, once small, now glaring with the light of madness." Branwell "looked frightened — frightened of himself," Grundy noted, but a couple of brandies and some dinner restored "something like the Brontë of old." When the time came to part, Grundy left his friend "standing bareheaded in the road, with bowed form and dropping tears."

Branwell was sicker than anyone imagined. Tuberculosis had taken hold in his lungs, and alcohol and opium had weakened his body and mind. A few days after Grundy's visit, on Sunday, September 24, with his family gathered around his bed, Branwell died. He was thirty-one years old. His sisters felt sorrow mixed with relief. "I do not weep from a sense of bereavement," Charlotte admitted, "but for the wreck of talent, the ruin of promise, the untimely dreary extinction of what might have been a burning and shining light." She added, "I had aspirations and ambitions for him once."

The Reverend Brontë had nurtured hopes for Branwell, too. Crying out, "My son! my son!" he rejected all comfort. "My poor father naturally thought more of his *only* son than of his daughters," Charlotte could not resist mentioning. Yet Francis Grundy thought that Patrick Brontë had let his son down. "That Rector of Haworth little knew how to bring up and bring out his clever family, and the boy least of all. He was a hard, matter-of-fact man," Grundy said. "So the girls worked their own way to fame and death, the boy to death only!" Branwell died knowing nothing of his sisters' literary success. "We could not tell him of our efforts for fear of causing him too deep a pang of remorse for his own time mis-spent, and talents misapplied," Charlotte said.

"Poor, brilliant, gay, moody, moping, wildly excitable, miserable Brontë!" Grundy lamented. "No history records your many struggles after the good, — your wit, brilliance, attractiveness, eagerness for excitement, — all the qualities which made you such 'good company,' and dragged you down to an untimely grave."

Branwell was barely laid to rest within the church at Haworth when Emily, and then Anne, showed signs of being ill. Their shortness of breath, constant coughing, and faint, speeding pulse pointed to tuberculosis. Emily appeared worse, but giving in to illness went against her nature. Even as she sickened and wasted away, Emily awoke at seven every morning and dressed herself. She went to bed at ten every night after putting in a full day of sewing, writing, practicing at the piano, and caring for the dogs. She permitted no "poisoning doctor" to come near her. Charlotte's anguish mixed with wonder as she watched Emily's iron will battling her weakening body. "I have seen nothing like it," Charlotte said; "but, indeed, I have never seen her parallel in anything."

On the night of December 18, 1848, Anne and Charlotte saw Emily stumble and nearly fall as she went out to feed the dogs. They hurried to help her, but Emily turned them away and finished her task. The next day, barely able to speak, Emily finally asked to see a doctor, but there was nothing he or anyone else could do. She died at two that afternoon. Some accounts say she died on the sofa in the parsonage dining room, whereas others state she was carried upstairs to bed and died there. Whether death found her on the sofa or in bed, her devoted dog Keeper was at her side. Emily Brontë was thirty years old and had grown so thin that her coffin measured only seventeen inches wide. The carpenter said he had never made a narrower one for an adult.

"Charlotte, you must bear up — I shall sink if you fail me," Patrick Brontë said to his older surviving daughter. Charlotte locked away her sorrow during the day for her father's sake, but it escaped at night, rousing her from sleep. Emily had been "torn from us in the fullness of our attachment, rooted up in the prime of her own days, in the promise of her powers," Charlotte wrote. Emily's early death, to Charlotte, was "like a field of green corn trodden down — like a tree in full bearing — struck at the root."

Then Anne came down with influenza at Christmas

Emily Brontë made this portrait of her beloved dog Keeper.

Emily Brontë is said to have died on the sofa in the dining room at Haworth parsonage, shown here as it looks today, but whether this is true is unknown.

and failed to get better in the new year. The flu aggravated her cough, which sounded just like Emily's, and she complained of a sharp pain in her side. Charlotte lost the will to write as she helplessly nursed Anne. She informed William Smith Williams of Smith, Elder and Company that Anne suffered through "nights of sleeplessness and pain, and days of depression and languor which nothing could cheer."

Patrick Brontë paid to have a specialist — an expert on consumption — come from Leeds to examine Anne. This medical man, Mr. Teale, prescribed cod liver oil and carbonate of iron, and he told Anne to get plenty of rest. He also consulted with the Reverend Brontë behind the closed door of the minister's office. All her father said afterward was, "My *dear* little Anne," but his few, simple words carried an ominous message.

Ellen Nussey was a visitor in the parsonage when the doctor came. To Ellen, who had guessed the true identities of Currer, Ellis, and Acton Bell, Anne looked "sweetly pretty and flushed and in capital spirits for an invalid." Anne dutifully took her medicine, although it made her sick to her stomach. Charlotte noted that it smelled and tasted "like train oil."

Anne admitted to her fears privately, in poetry, and asked God for courage:

> *I hoped, that with the brave and strong,*
> *   My portioned task might lie;*
> *To toil amid the busy throng,*
> *   With purpose pure and high.*

> *But God has fixed another part,*
> *   And He has fixed it well;*
> *I said so with my bleeding heart,*
> *   When first the anguish fell.*

A dreadful darkness closes in
On my bewildered mind;
Oh, let me suffer and not sin,
Be tortured, yet resigned.

Wanting a change of air, Anne talked of going to Scarborough, a vacation spot on the North Sea coast that she had visited as the Robinsons' governess. Mr. Teale approved the trip, and Ellen Nussey agreed to go along and help Charlotte with Anne's care. Ellen journeyed to Haworth on Wednesday, May 24. The next day, Anne said goodbye to her spaniel, Flossy, and to Emily's Keeper. The Reverend

Scarborough's scenic walkways and sandy beaches made it a popular vacation spot and spa among the Victorians.

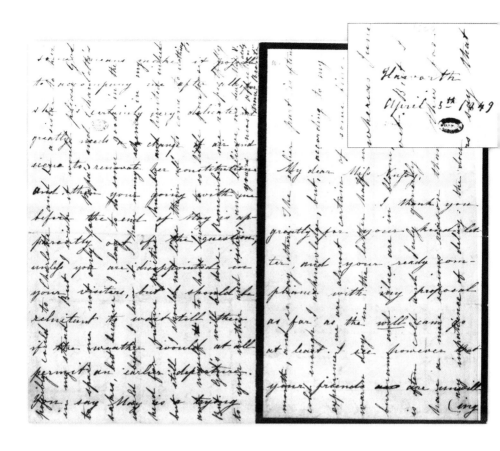

Anne Brontë wrote this letter inviting Ellen Nussey to come to Scarborough. Anne
employed a common practice called cross-hatching: after filling a page, she turned
it to the side and wrote perpendicularly across the first lines. Cross-hatching
allowed letter writers to save paper.

Brontë, Tabby, Martha, and the curate, Arthur Bell Nicholls, saw the women off, knowing they might never again
lay eyes on the living Anne. Nicholls held Flossy to prevent
her from running after the carriage.

Two days of train travel were exhausting for someone
as sick as Anne, but she remembered Emily's example and

drew on the little strength she had left to be a cheerful companion. In Scarborough she rode in a donkey cart to the beach and ventured with Charlotte and Ellen onto the Cliff Bridge, an iron span that offered sweeping views of Scarborough and beyond.

Spreading tuberculosis with every breath, Anne mingled with the healthy — with honeymooning couples and parents and young children. A deathly ill woman on holiday attracted less notice in the Brontës' time than she would today. The Victorians believed that sea air and a change of scene had healing effects, so the sick — even some with contagious diseases like tuberculosis — commonly visited the coast and mixed with healthy vacationers.

On Monday, May 28, Anne sat in a chair in their hotel room, looking out at the sea. She knew that she was dying. "Be a sister in my stead," she counseled Ellen. "Give Charlotte as much of your company as you can." When Anne grew too tired to sit, Ellen and Charlotte moved her to a sofa. "Take courage, Charlotte; take courage," Anne whispered as she saw her sister break down. A little while later, she died. Anne, dead at age twenty-nine, was buried in a Scarborough churchyard. She was the only Brontë not laid to rest in Haworth.

Four children had grown up together in the Haworth parsonage, turning to one another for friendship and support. Then, within the space of eight months, three had died. "A year ago — had a prophet warned me how I should stand in June 1849," Charlotte reflected, "had he foretold the autumn, the winter, the spring of sickness and suffering to be gone through — I should have thought — this can never be endured. It is over. Branwell — Emily — Anne are gone like dreams."

"Out of Obscurity I Came"

SOLITUDE, remembrance, and longing: these three shadowy companions settled themselves in Haworth, taking the places of Branwell, Emily, and Anne. Charlotte woke in the morning knowing they would be with her all day and keep her from a sound sleep at night. "Sometimes," she told Ellen Nussey, "I have a heavy heart of it." Yet she refused to be crushed. "I have many comforts — many mercies," she added. "Still I can *get on.*"

Charlotte clung to her writing as if it were a big, brawny friend, one with muscle enough to carry her through this current of sorrow. By September she could report a measure of progress to William Smith Williams: "Imagination lifted me when I was sinking, three months ago; its active exercise has kept my head above water since."

The work that pulled Charlotte out of her deepest grief was a new novel. Called *Shirley,* it was published in October 1849. *Shirley* was the kind of book that Mary Taylor liked best, because it dealt with social problems.

Charlotte set her story in Stillborough, a fictional Yorkshire town. She had it begin in 1811, when the Luddites were smashing up factories in northern England. As the novel opens, local mill owner Robert Moore plans to modernize his plant, but he has been threatened. To the region's working people, machines mean joblessness, hunger, and a loss of dignity. As one man remarks, "Invention may be all right, but I know it isn't right for poor folks to starve." After angry workers destroy Moore's new equipment, he vows to catch their leaders and bring them to justice. Moore needs machinery to stay in business. He knows that mechanization is bound to come, that even if the workers destroy his plant, other factories will take its place. He ignores the workers' suffering, though. "He never asked himself where those to whom he no longer paid weekly wages found daily bread," Brontë wrote.

In *Shirley,* Brontë also looked into the lives of women, among them Moore's distant cousin, Caroline Helstone. Caroline also lives in Stillborough. Her father is dead, and

Textile mills, like this one in Morley, were a common sight in the towns of northern England in the mid-1800s.

she knows nothing about her mother, who is thought to be alive. She was raised by her father's brother, a cold, unfeeling man who has done his duty by her. Caroline secretly loves Robert Moore but doubts he cares for her in return. She believes she may never marry, and wanting a purpose in life, she thinks about pursuing the only occupation open to her: being a governess. Her uncle rejects this idea. He shelters and feeds and clothes her, so Caroline has no need to work, he says. He cannot see how the dull, empty hours hang heavily on a healthy young woman. Caroline worries,

"What am I to do to fill the interval of time which spreads between me and the grave?"

Brontë cared so much about a woman's right to a full life that she stepped into the pages of *Shirley* to plead directly with the men of England: "Look at your poor girls, many of them fading around you, dropping off in consumption or decline; or, what is worse, degenerating to sour old maids,—envious, backbiting, wretched, because life is a desert to them." Worst of all for girls, Charlotte wrote, was having to act a part to gain a place in society through marriage. To the nation's fathers she wrote, "You would wish to be proud of your daughters and not to blush for them—then seek for them an interest and an occupation which shall raise them above the flirt, the maneuverer, the mischief-making tale-bearer."

Meanwhile, in Stillborough, another young woman has arrived. Shirley Keeldar owns property there, including an estate called Fieldhead. Her wealth gives her independence, which she cherishes. Shirley's face, Brontë wrote, "possessed a charm as well described by the word grace as any other. It was pale naturally, but intelligent, and of varied expression." Shirley has no parents and lives with a companion, Mrs. Pryor. This older woman had been Shirley's governess when the mistress of Fieldhead was a child.

A rich and beautiful woman like Shirley could easily attract a husband with money and a title, but she cares nothing about a man's wealth or high position. To be her husband, a man must have a sharp mind and a good character, and he must treat her as an equal. She will never be the "half doll, half angel" that many men want in a wife. To Victorian readers, Shirley's name symbolized the unusual freedom she enjoyed, which was like a man's: before 1849, Shirley was a man's name. But Shirley Keeldar made such a deep impression on some readers that they named their daughters after her. Before long, Shirley was transformed into a name for girls.

Shirley likes Caroline, and the two women become friends. Strong-minded and with a large dog at her side, Shirley represents Emily Brontë as Charlotte imagined she might be had she lived. Although Charlotte mourned both her sisters, she missed Emily more. "I let Anne go to God, and felt He had a right to her," she said. "I could hardly let Emily go. I wanted to hold her back then, and I want her back now." Devout Anne had seemed destined for Heaven, but Emily had been firmly of the earth.

A loan from Shirley helps Robert Moore fight back when workers launch an attack on his mill, and he makes sure its leaders are arrested. Robert has been spotted spending time with Shirley, and the people of Stillborough whisper that the two will be married. Caroline believes the rumor and grows ill. She steadily worsens, even under Mrs. Pryor's tender care, and some people fear the worst. Caroline rallies only when Mrs. Pryor reveals a secret: she is really Mrs. James Helstone, Caroline's mother.

Caroline needs her health to look in on Robert Moore, who has been shot by someone seeking revenge for the Luddites' arrest. By this time Robert has seen the squalid lives that many workers live, and he resolves to treat his employees well. Robert recovers as the government lifts the Orders in Council, reopening foreign markets to British manufacturers. Financially stable at last, he asks Caroline to be his wife.

The right husband for Shirley steps forward, too. He is someone who has known her for years and has long loved her. "Am I to die without you, or am I to live for you?" he asks. Shirley replies, "Die without me if you will. Live for me if you dare."

The critics praised *Shirley,* although some complained that it lacked *Jane Eyre*'s mystery and romance. Currer Bell's second novel delighted readers who had called the first one shocking and lurid, however. *Shirley* "enlists the purer sympathies of our nature, instead of appealing to its baser passions," noted a writer for the *Church of England Quarterly Review.* But was the author a woman or a man?

Charlotte Brontë may have lived a quiet, lonely life in remote Haworth, but the world was starting to figure out that she was Currer Bell. A rumor started in Keighley after someone at the post office opened a parcel for Charlotte from Smith, Elder and Company. Then Mary Taylor's brother Joe learned of her authorship and spread the word through his part of Yorkshire. Finally, one of Charlotte's old classmates from Roe Head recognized her in the pages of *Jane Eyre;* Currer Bell's descriptions of Lowood sounded too much like Charlotte Brontë's memories of Cowan Bridge to be a coincidence. This woman whispered her suspicion to the critic George Henry Lewes, and in his review of *Shirley* he identified the author as a clergyman's daughter. He then assessed the novel as a woman's book — doing just what Charlotte Brontë had guarded against. "The grand function of woman, it must always be recollected, is, and ever must be, Maternity," he proclaimed. The man was impossible!

Charlotte dashed off an angry letter to Lewes. "I wish all reviewers believed 'Currer Bell' to be a man — they would be more just to him," Charlotte wrote. "You will, I know, keep measuring me by some standard of what you deem becoming to my sex — where I am not what you consider graceful — you will condemn me." As a novelist she refused to decide whether every sentence she wrote sounded "elegant and charming in femininity." If society required this of her, then she would disappear from the world of books. "Out of obscurity I came," she warned. "To obscurity I can easily return."

With the truth becoming known, though, and with Anne and Emily gone, Charlotte had less reason to hide. When George Smith and his mother invited her to stay with them in London, she accepted. She hired a dressmaker to sew her a proper city wardrobe — in black, because she mourned. She was earning money from her books and could afford to leave her country dresses at home.

Smith's mother and sisters welcomed Charlotte politely, and soon their reserve softened into friendship. George Smith escorted Charlotte to art galleries and plays. He hosted a dinner party for her, with William Makepeace Thackeray among the guests. This celebrated novelist, who stood more than six feet tall, had "a peculiar face — not handsome — very ugly indeed," Charlotte wrote to her father. Thackeray was "stern in expression," she added, "but capable also of a kind look."

Thackeray was struck by Brontë's "trembling little frame, the little hand, the great honest eyes." No one told him of Charlotte's dual identity, but he figured out who she was. After dinner, when the men joined the women for coffee in the drawing room, as was the custom, he asked her if the "warning fragrance" of the gentlemen's cigars had announced their approach, as Edward Rochester had asked Jane Eyre.

Though Charlotte Brontë had dedicated the second edi-

William Makepeace Thackeray established himself as one of Victorian England's leading novelists with the publication of *Vanity Fair* in 1847.

tion of *Jane Eyre* to Thackeray, she admitted nothing that night. But she revealed herself a few days later to another celebrated writer, Harriet Martineau. A brilliant woman, Martineau had written books on education, economics, and travel. She had also authored a novel about a doctor, *Deerbrook,* that Charlotte had admired. When Charlotte learned that Martineau was staying with cousins in London, she wrote to request a meeting.

Martineau had read *Jane Eyre* and *Shirley* and had even exchanged notes with Currer Bell. Like many curious readers, she was dying to know Bell's identity. So she invited Mr. Bell to Sunday tea. "I lighted plenty of candles that we might see what manner of man or womankind it was, & we sat in wondering expectation," noted Lucy Martineau, one of Harriet's cousins.

Just before six there was a loud knock, and a man six feet tall strode into the room. He turned out to be a philanthropist who had come on some brief business, and Martineau wished he would finish it and be gone. No sooner did he leave than a carriage pulled up to the house, and a servant called out loudly, because Harriet Martineau had partial hearing loss, "Miss Brontë."

"I thought her the smallest creature I had ever seen (except at a fair)," wrote Martineau, who was tall, robust, and nearing fifty. "And her eyes blazed, as it seemed to me."

The writer Harriet Martineau befriended Charlotte Brontë, but the friendship was short-lived.

Seated beside Martineau on the sofa, Brontë "cast up at me such a look, — so loving, so appealing, — that, in connexion with her deep mourning dress," Martineau recalled, "I could with the utmost difficulty return her smile, or keep my composure. I should have been heartily glad to cry." Lucy Martineau volunteered, "She was so pleasant & so naïve, that is to say so innocent and un Londony that we were quite charmed with her." After tea the two authors chatted alone, with Brontë speaking loudly into the horn that Martineau held to her ear. Brontë turned "red all over with pleasure" to hear *Jane Eyre* praised, Martineau said.

Charlotte Brontë went to London again in June 1850. On this trip she and George Smith attended a party at Thackeray's home. Determined more than ever to make her reveal her secret, Thackeray introduced her to his other guests as Currer Bell. Charlotte corrected him smartly. According to another guest, she said that she "believed there were books being published by a person named Currer Bell . . . but the person he was talking to was Miss Brontë — and she saw no connection between the two." As soon as she could, Charlotte fled the drawing room, where the guests had gathered, and sat in the study with the Thackerays' governess. Miss Brontë "did not look pleasant," Thackeray's daughter Anne Ritchie recalled decades later. "I remember how she frowned at me whenever I looked at her."

Brontë also saw her hero, the Duke of Wellington, then

eighty-one years old, when Smith took her to the chapel where the great man worshiped on Sundays. Smith and Brontë followed Wellington down the steps when the service ended, and they passed him twice on their morning stroll. "He is a real grand old man," Charlotte said. On another day, she had lunch with George Henry Lewes, and he made her angry all over again by saying she had written "naughty books." George Smith listened "with mingled admiration and alarm" to the "explosion" that followed, as Brontë defended her work with "indignant eloquence." Later she told Ellen Nussey that she had trouble staying annoyed at Lewes, because his face was "so wonderfully like Emily."

While in London, Brontë sat for a portrait by George Richmond, who had studied art in Paris. Richmond created a flattering likeness of the novelist, emphasizing her soft, thick hair and soulful eyes. Her father's curate, Arthur Nicholls, went with Brontë to pick up the portrait when it was ready. As he admired the finished work, Brontë began to cry. "Oh, Mr. Richmond, it is so like Anne!" she said. When the portrait reached Haworth, Patrick Brontë declared that Richmond had captured the genius of the author of *Shirley* and *Jane Eyre*. Tabby Ayckroyd had a different opinion, however. She disliked the painting and complained that it made Charlotte look too old.

Charlotte Brontë made other trips that summer. She

The artist George Richmond created this flattering portrait of Charlotte Brontë. It has often been copied.

went to Scotland with George Smith and one of his sisters to pick up a brother who was in school there. She loved Edinburgh, the Scottish capital, and called her days there "as happy almost as any I ever spent." On a visit to a family named Kay-Shuttleworth, who had a home in Wordsworth's Lake Country, she befriended another guest, the novelist Elizabeth Gaskell. Brontë had read and admired Gaskell's novel *Mary Barton.* And Gaskell, a married woman who had lost a beloved son, had read *Jane Eyre* and *Shirley* and understood that their author, too, had known grief. On boat and country carriage rides, the two women talked about books and life. "She and I quarreled & differed about almost everything," Gaskell told another friend, "but we liked each other heartily." From Haworth Brontë sent Gaskell a "little book of rhymes": a copy of *Poems* by Currer, Ellis, and Acton Bell.

Then, in December, Charlotte spent "a *cosy* winter visit" with her other new friend, Harriet Martineau, at Martineau's stone house on Lake Windermere, England's largest lake. The energetic Martineau raised livestock and grew vegetables on her property. She took Brontë to meet the poet Matthew Arnold, who made a bad first impression. As he walked into the room with his chin held high, Brontë thought him to be self-important. Yet once she knew him better, she changed her mind. "Ere long a real modesty

In tune with the social issues of his time, the poet Matthew Arnold wrote in 1869, "My poems represent, on the whole, the main movement of mind of the last quarter of a century."

appeared under his assumed conceit," she decided. Arnold, for his part, saw Brontë only as "past thirty and plain, with expressive gray eyes, though."

Arnold's moving 1867 poem "Dover Beach" would capture the uncertainty of many Victorians as Darwin's writings on natural selection forced them to reconsider long-held beliefs:

> *Ah, love, let us be true*
> *To one another! for the world, which seems*
> *To lie before us like a land of dreams,*
> *So various, so beautiful, so new,*
> *Hath really neither joy, nor love, nor light,*
> *Nor certitude, nor peace, nor help for pain;*
> *And we are here as on a darkling plain*
> *Swept with confused alarms of struggle and flight,*
> *Where ignorant armies clash by night.*

One person who had rejected the faith of her forebears was Harriet Martineau. When she read aloud to Charlotte from a book she was writing, *Letters on the Law of Man's Social Nature and Development,* in which she championed atheism, Brontë hardly knew how to respond. "The strangest thing is that we are called on to rejoice over this hopeless blank," reflected Charlotte, who had known so much

In later life, Charlotte's old teacher Margaret Wooler exchanged her white dresses for darker garments.

grief, "to welcome this unutterable desolation as a pleasant state of freedom. Who could do this if he would? Who would do it if he could?"

Charlotte's own faith remained unshaken, and when her father, Ellen Nussey, and even Miss Wooler chided her for staying in the home of an admitted atheist, she defended her new friend. "My dear Miss Wooler—I believe if you were in my place, and knew Miss Martineau as I do—if you had shared with me the proofs of her rough but genuine kindness," she wrote, "you would be the last to give her up; you would separate the sinner from the sin."

While traveling and meeting well-known people like Harriet Martineau and Matthew Arnold, Charlotte Brontë no longer hid the fact that she was Currer Bell. A new edition of *Wuthering Heights* and *Agnes Grey* had just been published, for which Charlotte had written a "Biographical Notice of Ellis and Acton Bell." In this preface she told the world that the Bells were three sisters, and she revealed the names of Emily and Anne. Charlotte wrote, "For strangers they were nothing, for superficial observers less than nothing; but for those who had known them all their lives in the intimacy of close relationship, they were genuinely good and truly great."

ten

"I Should Fancy I Heard the Steps of the Dead"

*I*N January 1851, George Smith invited Charlotte Brontë to cruise with him on the Rhine River, which flows through modern-day Germany. Thoughts of travel always stirred up longing in Charlotte's soul, yet she worried that London would gossip. In the end, business forced Smith to cancel the plan, but Ellen Nussey sensed an "undercurrent" of feeling in his offer. She suspected that Smith had "fixed intentions" toward her friend.

Romance seemed likely when the Smiths asked Charlotte to spend time with them in London, starting at the end of May. Again she had new clothes made, but this time her eye went to airy colors — white and pastel pink — and not strictly mourning black. The visit began on a merry note, with Charlotte noting that her fourth day in London, June 1, was "very happy."

George Smith may not have seen beauty when he looked at Charlotte Brontë, but he was attracted to her mind. He twice took her to see the French actress Mademoiselle Rachel perform onstage. Acclaimed for her tragic roles, Rachel counted famous men, including an illegitimate son of Napoleon, among her many lovers. For Charlotte Brontë, Rachel on the stage was "a wonderful sight — 'terrible as if the earth had cracked deep at your feet.'"

Charlotte was also one of the six million Britons who toured the Great Exhibition of 1851, a proud celebration

A peddler's daughter, the performer known as Rachel first acted onstage to support her family. She died of tuberculosis in 1858, at age thirty-six.

of the triumphs of technology. Within the Crystal Palace, the mammoth glass building that housed the great display, people could see "every possible invention and appliance for the service of man," according to a guidebook, "every realization of human genius, every effort of human industry." The more than one hundred thousand exhibits had come from Britain and countries around the world. Visitors saw ores pulled from deep in the earth, machines that wove cotton cloth, timber from Canada, handcrafts from

Colorful rugs and textiles were on display in one section of London's Great Exhibition of 1851.

Tunisia, and a stuffed elephant from India. Charlotte went twice and told her father, "It seems as if magic only could have gathered this mass of wealth from all the ends of the Earth — as if none but supernatural hands could have arranged it thus — with such a blaze and contrast of colours and marvellous power of effect."

She again saw Thackeray, who needled her this time by greeting her in public as Jane Eyre. The next morning, when Thackeray called at the Smith home, Charlotte lambasted him for his ungentlemanly behavior. Thackeray left, having had enough of Charlotte Brontë. "There's a fire and fury raging in that little woman, a rage scorching her heart which doesn't suit me," he said.

By this time Charlotte's happiness had faded. Smith withdrew into his work and had little time for his guest. No one knows what went wrong, but Mrs. Smith opposed a relationship between Charlotte Brontë and her son and may have been to blame. Tuberculosis ran in the Brontë family, Mrs. Smith told George; this lone surviving sister was tainted with consumption. It was useless for Charlotte to insist that she was healthy; Mrs. Smith's mind was made up. Charlotte Brontë remained George Smith's friend, but she turned down an invitation to visit in September 1851 and another one that winter.

The thought that she was destined to live out her life in Haworth as her father's closest companion brought back her old friend depression. She worked at her writing, hoping to push the gloom from her mind. Then Emily's dog, Keeper, died, and Charlotte lost this link with a beloved sister. Soon, she had no appetite. Her head ached, and a pain shot through her side. A doctor diagnosed liver trouble and gave her blue pills to take, but they were full of mercury and nearly poisoned her. In spring she went to the Yorkshire coast to see Anne's grave, and walking in the sun and sea air helped to heal her body and spirit.

Arthur Nicholls came often to the parsonage. He chatted with the Reverend Brontë into the evening while Charlotte worked alone at the dining table. One night in December 1852, she heard Nicholls leave her father's study, but instead of going straight home, he tapped at the dining room door. "Like lightning it flashed on me what was coming," Charlotte wrote to Ellen. The curate stood before her, tall and solid, trembling from head to toe. All the color had drained from his face, and he was barely able to speak. With great trouble, he said that he had long cared for Charlotte and wanted her for his wife.

"He made me for the first time feel what it costs a man to declare affection where he doubts response," Charlotte wrote. "That he cared something for me — and wanted me to care for him — I have long suspected — but I did not know the degree or strength of his feelings."

Hardly knowing what to do, she guided the quaking

man from the room and promised him an answer the next day. Then, as a dutiful daughter, she put the matter before her father. "Papa worked himself into a state not to be tri-fled with — the veins on his temples started up like whip-cord — and his eyes became suddenly blood-shot," she reported. How dare an ordinary curate propose marriage to his talented daughter! And why did Nicholls address Charlotte without coming to her father first!

Charlotte told Ellen that if she had been in love with Nicholls, she never could have borne her father's furious oaths. As it was, the Reverend Brontë aroused her sense of fairness: the curate hardly deserved such abuse. For a single woman to go against her father's wishes was unseemly, so the next day, Charlotte answered Arthur Nicholls with a firm refusal and focused on her next novel, *Villette.*

More than ever before, Charlotte Brontë had drawn on her own life when writing *Villette,* which was published in 1853. She had studied her heart so that she could explore the inner life of her main character, an Englishwoman named Lucy Snowe. Lucy's name summed up the chilly spirit in which she began her life's adventure. Her heart slept under a white, wintry blanket. Lucy "has about her an external coldness," Brontë explained. The word "external" is important. Lucy only waits to have her inner fire kindled by love.

In *Villette,* Lucy tells her own story, as Jane Eyre did.

A tragedy — its nature unrevealed — has left her alone in the world, without family or home. At twenty-three, she claims to be "inadventurous, unstirred by impulses of practical ambition," yet almost on a whim she sails to Europe and becomes a teacher at a girls' school that is much like the Pensionnat Heger, in a fictional Belgian town called Villette. The school, housed in a building that used to be a convent, is rumored to be haunted by the ghost of a nun. Lucy, in her plain gray dress, resembles this shadowy spirit. Lucy's employer is Madame Beck, the headmistress who keeps tight order. Modeled on Madame Heger, Beck does her job with cool efficiency; "she had no heart to be touched," Lucy tells the reader.

Two men enter Lucy's life. The first is Dr. John, the handsome young English doctor who comes to the school to treat Madame Beck's children. Lucy eventually reveals to the reader that he is John Graham Bretton, her godmother's son, and someone she last saw in England a decade earlier. Throughout much of the novel, Dr. John is smitten with Ginevra Fanshawe, a coquette enrolled in the *pensionnat* where Lucy teaches. The other man is more suited to Lucy's mind and temperament. He is Monsieur Paul Emanuel, stern but kind, a fellow teacher who resembles Constantin Heger in looks and behavior. Through his friendship he draws Lucy out of her cold reserve, but she wonders what his feelings toward her might be.

Lucy is left virtually alone at the school during an end-of-summer vacation, and her solitude weighs heavily on her spirit. "My nervous system could hardly support what it had for many days and nights to undergo in that huge empty house," she says. She concludes that God plans for some people to live lives of suffering, "and I thrilled in the certainty that of this number I was one." Eventually, desperate for human contact, she enters the confessional in a Catholic church, as Charlotte Brontë had done. After leaving she suffers a breakdown and is rescued by Dr. John. He brings her to the home that he shares with his mother in Villette, and she recovers there. When Lucy is well enough, the doctor escorts her to the theater, where they see an actress much like Mademoiselle Rachel.

School resumes again, and the friendship deepens between Lucy Snowe and Paul Emanuel. Lucy continues to wonder how strongly he is attached to her. She gets her answer when a business matter requires him to travel to the West Indies for three years, and he asks her to marry him upon his return. He reveals that he has set up a school for her to run so that she can be independent and useful while he is away. "I had been left a legacy," Lucy says, "such a thought for the present, such a hope for the future, such a motive for a persevering, a laborious, an enterprising, a patient and brave course."

As Paul's date of return draws near, a wild storm barrels in from the southwest. "It did not cease till the Atlantic was strewn with wrecks: it did not lull till the deeps had gorged their fill of sustenance," Lucy relates. Does Monsieur Paul safely return? Brontë left this question for her readers to decide.

Most people liked *Villette* better than *Shirley.* Reviewers praised the author's "clear, forcible, picturesque style" and said the novel had the "charm of freshness." One eager writer claimed about Currer Bell, "This book would have made her famous, had she not been so already." Mary Ann Evans (the novelist George Eliot) read *Villette* three times. She pronounced it a "still more wonderful book than *Jane Eyre,*" and exclaimed about Brontë, "What passion, what fire in her!" A proud Patrick Brontë sent a copy of *Villette* to his brother in Ireland.

Some critics quibbled that parts of the book could have been better. One complained that the plot was "very slight"; another thought the author displayed a "cynical and bitter spirit." Brontë had learned to take such comments in stride, but she felt unable to forgive one particular review, because it came from Harriet Martineau. Writing in the *London Daily News,* Martineau had called *Villette* "almost intolerably painful." Not only does "an atmosphere of pain" hang over the story, but "all the female characters, in all their thoughts and lives, are full of one thing," Martineau wrote, and that one thing was love. Charlotte Brontë, who had long favored a woman's right to independence and ambition, had to bear the insult of this high-handed statement from Martineau: "There are substantial, heartfelt interests for women of all ages, and under ordinary circumstances, quite apart from love." Martineau also disliked the novel's main character, and said about Lucy Snowe, "We do not wonder that she loved more than she was beloved."

Stunned by this cruel betrayal, Charlotte sent a final letter to Martineau. "I know what *love* is as I understand it; and if a man or woman should be ashamed of feeling such love, then there is nothing right, noble, faithful, truthful, unselfish in this earth," she wrote.

"The differences of feeling between Miss M. and myself are very strong and marked; very wide and irreconcilable," she told George Smith. "In short she has hurt me a good deal, and at present it appears very plain to me that she and I had better not try to be close friends."

That spring, the time came for another parting. Arthur Nicholls had been a gloomy presence in Haworth since Charlotte refused him, and he had even broken down in tears during one Sunday's communion service. On the evening of May 26, Charlotte found him standing at the parsonage's garden gate, "in a paroxysm of anguish — sobbing as women never do," as she described him. He would soon start work at another church, but he could hardly bear the thought of leaving Haworth without seeing Charlotte once more. The two exchanged a few brief words. "Poor fellow!" Charlotte said. "He wanted such hope and such encouragement as I *could* not give him."

In September, when the purple heather that erupts on the moors had faded to brown, Charlotte's other writer friend, Elizabeth Gaskell, spent four days with her in Haworth. Charlotte cautioned Gaskell that she was coming to a place like "the backwoods of America." She was coming to a country of "barbarism, loneliness, and liberty," Charlotte warned.

A dull, gray village and strong gusts formed Gaskell's first impression of Haworth. Upon reaching the parsonage, she was "half-blown back by the wild vehemence of the wind which swept along the narrow walk," she wrote.

The novelist Elizabeth Cleghorn Gaskell was Charlotte Brontë's friend and first biographer.

Once inside, she received a kind welcome. She was given the bedroom that had been Aunt Branwell's, one that overlooked the graves in the churchyard. Gaskell, who saw life's bright side, claimed the view was "beautiful in certain lights."

Each day, the two women had breakfast and tea with Charlotte's father. Gaskell had trouble finding something good to say about the senior Brontë, though. She admitted to being "sadly afraid of him in my inmost soul; for I caught a glare of his stern eyes over his spectacles at Miss Brontë once or twice which made me know my man."

Out on the moors and in the parsonage after the others had gone to bed, Charlotte told Gaskell the story of her life. She talked about the school at Cowan Bridge, the tales of Angria, and her student years at Roe Head and in Brussels. She described the pain of losing Branwell, Emily, and Anne. After Gaskell retired for the night, Charlotte walked alone in the dining room as she once had walked with her sisters. Gaskell imagined how her friend must have felt. "I am sure I should fancy I heard the steps of the dead following me," she commented.

The passing months brought changes of circumstances and of heart. Patrick Brontë suffered a stroke that diminished the vision in his one good eye, and he needed his curate's help. Solitude weighed on Charlotte more heavily than ever, and her words lay dead on the page. So when

Arthur Nicholls came back to Haworth in January 1854 to assist the Reverend Brontë and to renew his offer to Charlotte, she approached the old man again. "Father, I am not a young girl, nor a young woman, even — I never was pretty," she said. But his response was the same: never. For an entire week after their discussion, he refused to say a word to her.

Finally, Tabby Aykroyd, the longtime household servant, lost patience and spoke up. "Do you wish to kill your daughter?" she demanded angrily of her employer. Patrick Brontë grudgingly gave in, and Charlotte and Arthur became engaged in March 1854.

Ellen Nussey disapproved. She spoke her mind in a letter to Mary Taylor in New Zealand, complaining that Nicholls was no match for someone like Charlotte. If Ellen expected a sympathetic reply, she was mistaken. Mary, who had decided against ever marrying herself, supported Charlotte's choice. "You talk wonderful nonsense," Mary shot back. Charlotte had every right to consider her own pleasure. "If this is so new for her to do, it is high time she began to make it more common," Mary wrote.

Mary was right: Charlotte was thinking of her own happiness. "I trust to love my husband. I am grateful for his tender love to me. I believe him to be an affectionate, a conscientious, a high-principled man," she wrote. She believed that Providence, or God's wise guidance, had opened this path for her. She would be lonely no more.

Charlotte Brontë and Arthur Nicholls were married on June 29, a Thursday. The bride wore a white embroidered dress and a white bonnet. The villagers of Haworth declared that she looked just like a snowdrop. The Reverend Brontë decided at the last minute not to give the bride away, so Miss Wooler did the honors. Ellen Nussey and the servants Tabby Aykroyd and Martha Brown were the only other guests.

The newlyweds honeymooned for a month in Arthur Nicholls's native Ireland. Charlotte met and liked his

Arthur Bell Nicholls won Charlotte Brontë's hand through persistence.

Charlotte Brontë was photographed in her last year of life.

family. She was surprised by the grandeur of their home, Cuba House, where Arthur had been raised by an uncle. She noted its thick walls, lofty rooms, and handsome furniture. Cuba House sat on ample grounds at the end of an avenue of lime trees. Everyone Charlotte met praised Arthur and told her she had married "one of the best gentlemen in the country." More than before, Charlotte was convinced that she had made "what seems to me a right choice."

Charlotte and Arthur returned to live in the Haworth parsonage, where Arthur took over many of the Reverend Brontë's duties. "Each time I see Mr. Nicholls put on gown or surplice — I feel comforted to think that this marriage has secured Papa good aid in his old age," Charlotte confided to Miss Wooler. She spent her days looking after her husband and father. She wrote no more novels, but she still wrote to her friends.

Arthur insisted on his right as a husband to read the letters exchanged between his wife and Ellen Nussey and to approve the ones that Charlotte wrote. But the two women hated to give up the intimacy they had enjoyed for so many years, and they protested. "Men don't seem to understand making letters a vehicle of communication — they always seem to think us incautious," Charlotte said. At last Arthur agreed to leave their correspondence alone if Ellen promised to burn Charlotte's letters — including those she had carefully saved over the years. Ellen swore that she would, but she had no intention of keeping this promise. Later she would claim that Nicholls had continued to censor what Charlotte wrote to her. If he broke his side of the bargain, then she was under no obligation to uphold hers. (Either Charlotte or Arthur destroyed the letters that Ellen wrote.)

December came, and Charlotte believed she was pregnant, if the nausea she felt was any clue. Instead of passing, though, her queasiness worsened. She grew feverish and frail and went to bed. A week, two weeks, and more passed, and she felt no better. Tabby Aykroyd was sick, too. When Tabby died, on February 17, 1855, at eighty-four, Charlotte was still bedridden and was vomiting blood. The local doctors had no idea what was wrong. They spoke of phthisis, or wasting away, and tuberculosis.

By the third week in March, Charlotte was fading in and out of consciousness, but in an alert moment she heard Arthur ask God to spare her. "Oh! I am not going to die, am I?" she cried. "He will not separate us; we have been so happy." She managed to scrawl a last note to her friends: "No kinder, better husband than mine, it seems to me, there can be in the world." Ellen Nussey rushed to Haworth, but she was too late to say goodbye. Instead she prepared her friend's body for burial. Charlotte Brontë had died on March 31, 1855. In three weeks she would have turned thirty-nine.

Afterword

"ALAS!"

Early she goes on the path
To the Silent Country, and leaves
Half her laurels unwon,
Dying too soon . . .

Currer Bell—Charlotte Brontë—was dead. Matthew Arnold had been moved to remember her in verse when he learned that she was gone.

Other tributes appeared in print, including a mean-spirited one from Harriet Martineau, in which she repeated her criticism of Brontë's novels. "Her heroines love too readily, too vehemently, and sometimes after a fashion which their female readers may resent," Martineau wrote.

She reminded people of what had shocked them in the 1840s about all three Bells: "the coarseness which, to a certain degree, pervades the works of all the sisters, and the repulsiveness which makes the tales by Emily and Anne really horrible to people who have not iron nerves."

Martineau was smart enough to recognize that her late friend's talent was greater than her own. Her words smack of jealousy, especially her final image of Currer Bell as a passing literary fad, soon to be forgotten. Bell had already become a shadow, Martineau wrote, "vanishing from our view."

The people who had loved Charlotte Brontë hated to see her or her sisters remembered as crude or unnatural, so the Reverend Patrick Brontë appealed to Elizabeth Gaskell. "I can see no better plan, under these circumstances, than to apply to some established Author, to write a brief account of her life," he wrote. "You, seem to me, to be the best qualified, for doing what I wish should be done."

Gaskell took on the job. She returned to Haworth and spoke with Charlotte's still-tearful husband and father. Patrick Brontë trusted her with the tiny books Charlotte had created as a child and some of her letters to the family. Gaskell also read the many letters that Ellen Nussey had saved. She interviewed Margaret Wooler, and she corresponded with Mary Taylor, who regretted destroying her letters from Charlotte. Gaskell even tracked down the Hegers in

Belgium. Constantin Heger offered her Charlotte's student compositions, but his wife, angry about how she was portrayed in *Villette,* wanted nothing to do with the project.

The Life of Charlotte Brontë was published in 1857, two years after its subject's death. Gaskell's Brontë was like Jane Eyre, a small, virtuous woman who had struggled against sorrow and hardship. Her painful experiences, rather than a morbid imagination, had shaped her work. Gaskell mentioned nothing about Charlotte's love for Monsieur Heger, of which few Victorians would have approved.

Many people throughout Great Britain were curious about the minister's daughters from Haworth who had written such powerful fiction, so they bought the book. Gaskell's popular biography changed the public's opinion

Brontë's friend Mary Taylor returned to England in 1860. She finally finished her novel, *Miss Miles,* and published it in 1890.

of the Brontës. It became acceptable even for ladies to view the sisters in a sympathetic light. Tourists made pilgrimages to Haworth, to walk on its steep main street and see the scenes of the Brontës' lives, as admirers still do today. Far-off fans wrote to Patrick Brontë to ask for samples of Charlotte's handwriting. He obliged by cutting up many of her letters and mailing off the pieces.

Another book that came out in 1857 attracted less attention. Smith, Elder and Company at last published *The Professor,* the first book that Charlotte Brontë wrote and her only novel whose main character is male. In this book it is a young Englishman who becomes a teacher in a Belgian girls' school. He falls in love with a student, a Swiss orphan with an English mother. Charlotte Brontë had written *The Professor* when she still had feelings for Constantin Heger. She gave this teacher and pupil the happy ending that life had denied her.

In the Haworth parsonage, life went quietly and sadly on. Patrick Brontë bought a dog, a Newfoundland-retriever mix named Cato, because his "Dear Daughter Charlotte" had admired him. A year after Charlotte's death, he wrote, "My grief is so deep and lasting, that I cannot long dwell on my sad privation — I try to look to God, for consolation, and pray that he will give me grace, and strength equal to my day — and resignation to his will."

Patrick Brontë died in his bed on June 7, 1861, with

Martha Brown and Arthur Nicholls at his side. Five months later, Nicholls moved back to Ireland and became a gentleman farmer. He married again, and he lived until 1906.

By then *Jane Eyre* was already considered a classic. Its story is timeless, but how people interpret it reflects the period in which they live. Today's readers are more interested in psychology than in questions of right and wrong, so modern scholars have studied how *Jane Eyre* portrays the workings of the mind. The author Nina Auerbach, for example, has said that Thornfield Hall mirrors "Jane's inner world," that it is the place where her deepest fears and desires are played out. The women's movement has also shaped the modern understanding of *Jane Eyre*. To

The Reverend Patrick Brontë, photographed in old age, outlived all his children. He died in 1861, at age eighty-four. The merchants in Haworth closed their shops on the day of his funeral.

poet Adrienne Rich, Jane's statement that her feelings are just like a man's is "Charlotte Brontë's feminist manifesto."

The world has also acknowledged Emily Brontë's great achievement in *Wuthering Heights*. Although Victorian readers tried to decide if Heathcliff was a demon or a man, today people view him symbolically. He may symbolize the untamed side of Catherine's nature, which she tried to deny when she became an adult. Heathcliff has also been called an example of an archetype, or a character that reappears in literature throughout the ages. The archetype's name and circumstances vary, but he or she always plays a similar role. To Professor Patricia Meyer Spacks, Heathcliff is the rebellious young male who refuses to obey society's rules. "Give him a black leather jacket and a motorcycle and he'd fit right into many a youthful dream even now," she has written.

Contemporary readers also looked closely at Anne Brontë's books, which were long overshadowed by her sisters' more famous work. They have discovered a writer with real insight into human relationships, and some have said that Anne Brontë might have gone on to be the greatest novelist of the three if she had lived.

But such thoughts can only be speculation, because all three sisters died so young. "Strew with roses the grave / Of the early-dying," wrote Matthew Arnold. "Alas!"

Notes

one: "OH GOD, MY POOR CHILDREN!"

3 Patrick Brontë, "Where Sin abounds . . ." is from "Winter-Night Meditations," in Turner, p. 40.

4 Maria Branwell Brontë, "Oh God, my poor children!" is quoted in Gordon, p. 8.

4 Patrick Brontë, "I was left quite alone" is quoted in "Patrick Brontë Chronology."

6 "altogether clever of her age" and "read prettily" are quoted in Gordon, p. 15.

7 Wilson, "Sin, like a full-blown weed . . ." is from Wilson, p. 21.

9 Maria Brontë, "God waits only the separation . . ." is quoted in Gordon, pp. 16–17.

9 "graveyard cough" is from Dormandy, p. 22.

10 "Long, long, long ago . . ." is from "Christmas Dreams," p. 1.

12 Wordsworth, "Nature never did betray . . ." is from "Tintern Abbey," in Abrams, p. 1376

12 Byron, "mingle with the Universe . . ." is from "Childe Harold's Pilgrimage," in Abrams, p. 1626.

13   Charlotte Brontë, "Flowers brighter than the rose . . ." is quoted in Willy, p. 120.

14   Patrick Brontë, "very little about herself . . ." is quoted in Gordon, p. 11.

15   Anne Brontë, "I see, far back . . ." is from "Self-Communion," in Chitham, p. 153.

15   Charlotte Brontë, "I am in the kitchen . . ." is from Beer, p. 181.

16   Emily Brontë, "Anne and I have been peeling apples . . ." is quoted in Rees, p. 33.

16   Charlotte Brontë, "I snatched one up . . ." is quoted in Alexander 1983, p. 27.

18   Branwell Brontë, "Crying, 'I have done . . .'" is quoted in Collins, p. xxix.

19   Emily Brontë, "Come, the wind may never again . . ." is from "D.G.C. to J.A.," in Emily Brontë 1989, p. 17.

two: "BEND INCLINATION TO DUTY"

21   Charlotte Brontë, "When you are a little depressed . . ." is quoted in Gordon, p. 42.

22   Nussey, "She had ever the demeanour . . ." is quoted in Shorter 1908, vol. 1, p. 85.

23   Wooler, "Bend inclination to duty," is quoted in Gordon, p. 39.

24   Charlotte Brontë, "a fine, generous soul . . ." is quoted in Gordon, p. 147.

24   Taylor, "things that were out of our range . . ." is from Stevens, p. 158.

24   Taylor, "She picked up every scrap . . ." is from Stevens, p. 163.

24   Nussey, "she chose in many things . . ." is quoted in Shorter 1908, vol. 1, p. 86.

25 Nussey, "all told in a voice . . ." is quoted in Shorter 1908, vol. 1, p. 88.

26 Nussey, "Branwell had probably never been far . . ." is quoted in Rees, p. 40.

28 Charlotte Brontë, "In one delightful, though somewhat monotonous . . ." is from Wise, vol. 1, p. 103.

28, 29 Nussey, "inseparable companions," "in the very closest sympathy . . ." and "lithesome, graceful figure" are from Wise, vol. 1, p. 112.

29 Nussey, "Sometimes they looked grey . . ." is quoted in Barker, p. 194.

29 Nussey, "One of her rare expressive looks . . ." is quoted in Gordon, p. 43.

29 Nussey, "had lovely violet-blue eyes . . ." is from Wise, vol. 1, p. 112.

29 Nussey, "strange stories . . ." is from Wise, vol. 1, p. 114.

31 Branwell Brontë, "I *know* that I am not one . . ." and "Now Sir, to you I appear . . ." are from Wise, vol. 1, p. 134.

31 Charlotte Brontë, "Must I from day to day sit . . ." is quoted in Gordon, p. 52.

31 Charlotte Brontë, "dolts," is quoted in Gordon, p. 49.

32 Charlotte Brontë, "quivering & shaking with stars," is from Alexander 2010, p. 156.

32 Charlotte Brontë, "What in all this is there . . ." is quoted in Rees, p. 52.

32 Charlotte Brontë, "I could have been no better . . ." is from Wise, vol. 2, p. 117.

32 Charlotte Brontë, "Liberty was the breath . . ." is from *The Works of Charlotte, Emily and Anne Brontë,* vol. 8, pp. 148–49.

33 Anne Brontë, "This place of solitude . . ." is from Chitham, p. 60.

33 Southey, "Literature cannot be the business . . ." is from Wise, vol. 1, p. 155.

34 Charlotte Brontë, "I have endeavoured . . ." is quoted in Gordon, p. 65.

35 Charlotte Brontë, "Am I to spend . . ." is quoted in Gordon, p. 67.

35 Charlotte Brontë, "I told her one or two rather plain truths . . ." and "If anybody likes me . . ." are quoted in Rees, pp. 61–62.

36 Charlotte Brontë, "There is a climax . . ." is from Charlotte Brontë, *The Professor, Emma and Poems,* p. 26.

36 Charlotte Brontë, "My health and spirits . . ." is from Wise, vol. 1, p. 166.

36 Charlotte Brontë, "Mary is playing . . ." is from Wise, vol. 1, p. 167.

38 Patrick Brontë, "Should a flea . . ." is quoted in Lock and Dixon, p. 383.

38 Patrick Brontë, "A roasted onion . . ." is quoted in Lock and Dixon, p. 382.

three: "WHAT ON EARTH IS HALF SO DEAR?"

39 Charlotte Brontë, "I fear she will never stand it," is from Wise, vol. 1, p. 162.

39 "though she could not easily associate . . ." is quoted in Barker, p. 294.

40 Emily Brontë, "There is a spot . . ." is from Emily Brontë, *The Complete Poems of Emily Jane Brontë,* p. 94.

41, 42 "low in stature . . ." and "He was a very steady . . ." are quoted in Rees, p. 63.

43 Charlotte Brontë, "in a common-sense style . . ." and "Do I love him . . ." are from Wise, vol. 1, p. 174.

43 Charlotte Brontë, "You do not know me . . ." is from Shorter 1896, p. 295.

44 Charlotte Brontë, "I had a kindly leaning . . ." is from Wise, vol. 1, p. 174.

47   "the usual branches . . ." is quoted in Howe, p. 113.

48   Charlotte Brontë, "desperate little dunces," is from Wise, vol. 1, p. 175.

48   Ingham, "had once employed a very unsuitable governess . . ." is quoted in Whitehead, p. 84.

48, 49 Charlotte Brontë, "More riotous, perverse, unmanageable cubs . . ." and "does not intend to know me" are from Wise, vol. 1, p. 178.

50   Ellis, "Gentlemen may employ their hours . . ." is from Ellis, p. 266.

51   "She may be known . . ." is quoted in Howe, p. 112.

51   Charlotte Brontë, "I am tolerably well convinced . . ." is from Wise, vol. 1, p. 206.

52   "owes its fame to its commerce" is from Smithers, p. 78.

52   Charlotte Brontë, "the idea of seeing the SEA . . ." is from Wise, vol. 1, p. 183.

52   Charlotte Brontë, "Its glorious changes . . ." is from Shorter 1896, p. 299.

53   Nussey, "There never could have been . . ." is quoted in Gordon, p. 82.

53, 54 Branwell Brontë, "farewell of old friend whisky" and "a native of the land . . ." are quoted in Barker, p. 320.

54, 55 Branwell Brontë, "I take neither spirits, wine nor malt liquors . . ." and "two days out of every seven" are quoted in Barker, p. 322.

56   Patrick Brontë, "agreeable in person . . ." is from Turner, p. 258.

57   Charlotte Brontë, "Miss Celia Amelia Weightman" is from Wise, vol. 1, p. 201.

57   Charlotte, Emily, and Anne Brontë, "Believe us when we frankly say . . ." is from Barker, p. 325.

57   Charlotte Brontë, "sits opposite to Anne . . ." is quoted in Chitham, p. 15.

59   Grundy, "small and thin of person . . ." is from Grundy, p. 75.

four: "Who Ever Rose . . . Without Ambition?"

60   Charlotte Brontë, "No one but myself can tell . . ." is quoted in Barker, p. 351.

61   Emily Brontë, "A scheme is at present in agitation . . ." is from Shorter 1896, p. 147.

61   Anne Brontë, "what will be our condition . . ." is from Orel, p. 45.

61   Emily Brontë, "all merrily seated . . ." is from Shorter 1896, p. 147.

62   Charlotte Brontë, "Papa will perhaps think it . . ." and "he was as ambitious . . ." are from Wise, vol. 1, p. 242.

62   Charlotte Brontë, "Before our half year . . ." is from Shorter 1896, p. 92.

64   Charlotte Brontë, "a little black ugly being . . ." is from Wise, vol. 1, p. 260.

64   "In talking perhaps . . ." is quoted in Gordon, p. 97.

64   Heger, "sacrifice, *without pity* . . ." is from Hoar, p. 216.

65   Charlotte Brontë, "The bird's nest is but a line . . ." is from Hoar, p. 214.

65   Emily Brontë, "He is inwardly convinced . . ." is from Lonoff, p. 98.

65   Heger, "a head for logic . . ." is quoted in Barker, p. 392.

66   Charlotte Brontë, "Emily works like a horse," and "this time she rallied . . ." are quoted in Barker, p. 384.

66   Emily Brontë, "I wish to be . . ." is from Lonoff, p. xli.

67   Taylor, "not only in health . . ." is quoted in Stevens, p. 38.

67   Wheelwright, "I simply disliked her . . ." and "Charlotte was so devotedly attached . . ." are quoted in Barker, p. 395.

68   Charlotte Brontë, "We are completely isolated . . ." is from Wise, vol. 1, p. 260.

69   Patrick Brontë, "saw him in tranquility . . ." is from Turner, p. 259.

70   Anne Brontë, "If few and short . . ." is from Chitham, p. 87.

70   "orthodox principles . . ." is from *Haworth Village*. Available online. URL: www.haworth-village.org.uk/hostiry/church/inside_church.asp. Downloaded on January 16, 2011.

71   Charlotte Brontë, "was to her more . . ." and "calm and serious . . ." are from Stevens, p. 41.

71   Branwell Brontë, "I have now lost . . ." is from Wise, vol. 1, p. 273.

72   Branwell Brontë, *"almost insanity"* and "I can now speak . . ." are from Wise, vol. 1, pp. 263–64.

73   Branwell Brontë, "Shall this pale Corpse . . ." is from Neufeldt, p. 229.

74   Charlotte Brontë, "an irresistible impulse," is quoted in Gordon, p. 106.

75   Charlotte Brontë, "It seems you will hardly hear . . ." is quoted in Barker, p. 411.

75   Charlotte Brontë, "Throughout my early youth . . ." is from Lonoff, p. 362.

78   "He was a worshipper . . ." is quoted in Barker, p. 419.

78   Charlotte Brontë, "I actually did confess . . ." is from Wise, vol. 1, p. 304.

five: "A Peculiar Music"

81   Charlotte Brontë, "I suffered much . . ." is from Wise, vol. 2, p. 3.

81   Charlotte Brontë, "Oh it is certain . . ." is from Wise, vol. 2, p. 14.

83   Anne Brontë, "had some very unpleasant . . ." is from Orel, p. 73.

83   Charlotte Brontë, "bad beyond expression," is from Wise, vol. 2, p. 43.

83 Branwell Brontë, "My mistress is DAMNABLY TOO FOND . . ." is quoted in Barker, p. 459.

84 Branwell Brontë, "ripened into declarations . . ." and "mental and personal attractions . . ." are from Grundy, p. 87.

85 Charlotte Brontë, "No one in the house . . ." is from Wise, vol. 2, p. 43.

85 Branwell Brontë, "a certain woman . . ." is quoted in Leyland, p. 76.

85 Emily Brontë, "During our excursion . . ." is from Wise, vol. 2, pp. 49–51.

86 Taylor, "I told her very warmly . . ." is quoted in Stevens, p. 161.

86 "a more promising career . . ." is from Ward, p. 1.

86 Charlotte Brontë, "I intend to stay," is quoted in Stevens, p. 161.

86 Charlotte Brontë, "You showed me once . . ." is quoted in Gordon, p. 116.

86 Charlotte Brontë, "the slave of a regret . . ." is quoted in Gordon, p. 119.

88 Charlotte Brontë, "He appears a respectable young man . . ." is from Wise, vol. 2, p. 35.

88 Brown, "Many's the time . . ." is quoted in Scruton, p. 130.

89 Charlotte Brontë, "something more than surprise . . ." and "these verses too . . ." are from Charlotte Brontë, "Biographical Notice of Ellis and Acton Bell," p. 6.

91 Vivian [Lewes], "Does it never strike . . ." is from Vivian, "A Gentle Hint to Writing-Women," p. 189.

91 Emily Brontë, "a hopeless being," and Charlotte Brontë, "In his present state . . ." are from Wise, vol. 2, p. 84.

92 Charlotte Brontë, "Some have won a wild delight . . ." is from Bell, Bell, and Bell, p. 112.

92 Charlotte Brontë, "The human heart has hidden treasures . . ." is from Bell, Bell, and Bell, p. 121.

92 Emily Brontë, "Oh, stars, and dreams . . ." is from Bell, Bell, and Bell, p. 23.

92 Emily Brontë, "Cold in the earth . . ." is from Bell, Bell, and Bell, p. 31.

93 Anne Brontë, "If life must be so full . . ." is from Bell, Bell, and Bell, p. 81.

93 Anne Brontë, "My soul is awakened . . ." is from Bell, Bell, and Bell, p. 125.

94 "the bleating of a calf," is from Gaskell, p. 261.

94 Charlotte Brontë, "To papa he allows rest . . ." is quoted in Barker, p. 493.

94 Patrick Brontë, "only some little effect," is quoted in Lock and Dixon, p. 381.

95, 96 "a ray of sunshine . . . ," "a fine quaint spirit . . . ," and "Perhaps they desired . . ." are quoted in Barker, p. 497.

97 Charlotte Brontë, "She does her business . . ." is from Wise, vol. 3, p. 99.

99 Patrick Brontë, "The feeling, under the operation . . ." is quoted in Barker, p. 507.

100 Charlotte Brontë, "a heroine as small and as plain . . ." is quoted in Allott, p. 303.

six: "It Is Soul Speaking to Soul"

102 Branwell Brontë, "Constant and unavoidable depression . . ." is from Wise, vol. 2, p. 114.

102 Charlotte Brontë, "The sky looks like ice . . ." is from Wise, vol. 2, p. 117.

105 Charlotte Brontë, "Were I to retrench . . ." is quoted in Barker, p. 528.

105 Charlotte Brontë, "There was no possibility . . ." is from C. Brontë, *Jane Eyre*, p. 39.

106   Eyre [Charlotte Brontë], "My Uncle Reed is in heaven . . ." is from C. Brontë, *Jane Eyre*, p. 60.

106   Charlotte Brontë, "a black pillar" and "like a carved mask," are from C. Brontë, *Jane Eyre*, p. 63.

106   Brocklehurst [Charlotte Brontë], "When you put bread . . ." is from C. Brontë, *Jane Eyre*, p. 95.

108   Scatcherd [Charlotte Brontë], "You dirty, disagreeable girl . . ." is from C. Brontë, *Jane Eyre*, p. 85.

108   Burns [Charlotte Brontë], "Love your enemies . . ." is from C. Brontë, *Jane Eyre*, p. 90.

109   Eyre [Charlotte Brontë], "I was no Helen Burns," is from C. Brontë, *Jane Eyre*, p. 98.

109   Charlotte Brontë, "I abstained from recording . . ." is from Wise, vol. 2, p. 150.

109   Eyre [Charlotte Brontë], "women feel just as men feel . . ." is from C. Brontë, *Jane Eyre*, p. 141.

110   Rochester [Charlotte Brontë], "heart-weary and soul-withered," is from C. Brontë, *Jane Eyre*, p. 247.

110   Eyre [Charlotte Brontë], "warning fragrance," is from C. Brontë, *Jane Eyre*, p. 276.

110   Rochester [Charlotte Brontë], "Don't long for poison . . ." is from C. Brontë, *Jane Eyre*, p. 290.

110   Charlotte Brontë, "demoniac laugh," is from C. Brontë, *Jane Eyre*, p. 179.

111   Thackeray, "It interested me so much . . ." is from Wise, vol. 2, p. 149.

112   Lewes, "It is soul . . ." is from Lewes, p. 691.

113   Lewes, "The writer is evidently a woman . . ." is from Lewes, pp. 690–91.

113   "a novel of remarkable power . . ." is from "An Evening's Gossip on New Novels," p. 614.

114 "Why, they have got Cowan Bridge School . . ." and Charlotte Brontë, "He did not recognize Currer Bell . . ." are quoted in Gordon, p. 164.

114 Taylor, "so perfect as a work of art . . ." is from Stevens, p. 74.

115 Charlotte Brontë, "Papa, I have been writing . . ." is from Wise, vol. 3, p. 144.

115 Patrick Brontë, "I hope you have not been . . ." is from Wise, vol. 3, p. 144.

115 Charlotte Brontë, "I think I shall gain . . ." is from Wise, vol. 3, p. 144.

115 Patrick Brontë, "Children, Charlotte has been writing . . ." is from Wise, vol. 3, p. 144.

115 "In 'Jane Eyre' the immorality . . ." is from "The Last New Novel," p. 377.

115 "Religion is stabbed . . ." is from "The Last New Novel," p. 380.

115 "It would be no credit . . ." is from "The Last New Novel," p. 376.

115 Rigby, "the personification of an unregenerate . . ." and "is the strength . . ." are from Gates, p. 139.

116 Rigby, "for if we ascribe . . ." is from Gates, pp. 141–142.

116 Rigby, "if by no woman . . ." is from Gates, p. 142.

116 Charlotte Brontë, "in whose eyes . . ." is from C. Brontë, *Jane Eyre*, p. 35.

seven: "MOORISH, AND WILD, AND KNOTTY AS A ROOT OF HEATH"

118 Emily Brontë, "dark almost as if it came . . ." is from E. Brontë, *Wuthering Heights,* p. 30.

119 Catherine Linton [Emily Brontë], "I'm wearying to escape . . ." is from E. Brontë, *Wuthering Heights,* p. 137.

120 Catherine Linton [Emily Brontë], "You have killed me . . ." is from E. Brontë, *Wuthering Heights,* p. 135.

120 Heathcliff, "You have killed yourself . . ." is from E. Brontë, *Wuthering Heights*, p. 137.

122 Charlotte Brontë, "It is moorish . . ." is quoted in Gordon, p. 150.

122 "The characters are as false . . ." and "a perfect pandemonium . . ." are from "Noteworthy Novels," p. 486.

122 "took the liberty . . ." is from "Noteworthy Novels," p. 486.

122, 123 Emily Brontë, "strange wild pictures" and "heightening their repulsiveness" are from "Wuthering Heights," p. 953.

123, 124 "that they have never read . . ." and "We must leave it . . ." are from Allott, p. 228.

124 "to put every trust . . ." is quoted in Alexander and Smith, p. 10.

124 Anne Brontë, "Such humble talents . . ." is quoted in Harrison and Stanford, p. 238.

124 Anne Brontë, "All true histories . . ." is from A. Brontë, *Agnes Grey*, p. 1.

124, 125 "subjects that are peculiar . . ." and "the injudicious selection . . ." are quoted in Alexander and Smith, p. 9.

125 "must have bribed some governess . . ." is from Allott, p. 227.

125 Grey [Anne Brontë], "How delightful it would be . . ." and "to earn my own maintenance . . ." are from A. Brontë, *Agnes Grey*, p. 7.

126 Mrs. Bloomfield [Anne Brontë], "the flower of the flock . . ." is from A. Brontë, *Agnes Grey*, p. 12.

126 Grey [Anne Brontë], "oblige, instruct, refine . . ." and "render them as superficially attractive . . ." are from A. Brontë, *Agnes Grey*, p. 45.

127 Rosalie Ashby [Anne Brontë], "And as for all the wisdom . . ." is from A. Brontë, *Agnes Grey*, p. 135.

128 Grey [Anne Brontë], "Of course, I pitied her . . ." is from A. Brontë, *Agnes Grey*, p. 134.

132   Smith, "rather quaintly dressed . . ." is from Smith, p. 89.

133   Smith, "country cousins," is from Stevens, p. 177.

133   Charlotte Brontë, "he would have liked some excitement" is from Stevens, p. 179.

133   Charlotte Brontë, "Fine ladies and gentlemen . . ." is from Stevens, pp. 179–80.

134   Charlotte Brontë, "a firm, intelligent man . . ." is from Stevens, p. 181.

134, 135   Smith, "interesting rather than attractive . . ." and "was a gentle, quiet, rather subdued person . . ." are from Smith, p. 91.

136   Helen Huntingdon [Anne Brontë], "destitute of principle . . ." is from A. Brontë, *The Tenant of Wildfell Hall,* p. 109.

136   "There are scenes . . ." is from "Noteworthy Novels," pp. 486–87.

136   Helen Huntingdon [Anne Brontë], "Mr. Hattersley burst into the room . . ." is from A. Brontë, *The Tenant of Wildfell Hall,* pp. 219–20.

137   Helen Huntingdon [Anne Brontë], "Without another word . . ." is from A. Brontë, *The Tenant of Wildfell Hall,* p. 171.

137   Sinclair, "The slamming of that bedroom door . . ." is from Sinclair, p. 48.

138   Arthur Huntingdon [Anne Brontë], "make a man of him," is from A. Brontë, *The Tenant of Wildfell Hall,* p. 280.

139   Blackstone, "In law, the husband and wife . . ." is quoted in Chaplin, p. 35.

139   Arthur Huntingdon [Anne Brontë], "What is God . . ." is from A. Brontë, *The Tenant of Wildfell Hall,* p. 364.

140   "There seems in the writer . . ." is from Allott, p. 250.

140   Anne Brontë, "If there were less . . ." is quoted in Alexander and Smith, p. 496.

140   Anne Brontë, "If I have warned . . ." is quoted in Alexander and Smith, p. 498.

140   Charlotte Brontë, "Papa—and sometimes all of us . . ." is from Wise, vol. 2, p. 240.

141   Grundy, "He spoke of Branwell . . ." is from Grundy, pp. 90–91.

141   Grundy, "was a mass of red, unkempt, uncut hair . . .", "looked frightened . . .", and "something like the Brontë of old," are from Grundy, p. 91.

141   Grundy, "standing bareheaded in the road . . ." is from Grundy, p. 92.

142   Charlotte Brontë, "I do not weep . . ." is from Wise, vol. 2, p. 261.

142   Patrick Brontë, "My son! my son!" and Charlotte Brontë, "My poor father naturally thought . . ." are from Shorter, p. 99.

142   Grundy, "That Rector of Haworth . . ." is from Grundy, p. 74.

142   Charlotte Brontë, "We could not tell him . . ." is from Shorter, p. 139.

142   Grundy, "Poor, brilliant, gay, moody . . ." is from Grundy, p. 74.

143   Emily Brontë, "poisoning doctor," and Charlotte Brontë, "I have seen nothing like it . . ." are quoted in Gordon, p. 185.

144   Patrick Brontë, "Charlotte, you must bear up . . ." is from Wise, vol. 2, p. 295.

144   Charlotte Brontë, "torn from us in the fullness of our attachment . . ." is from Wise, vol. 2, p. 295.

145   Charlotte Brontë, "nights of sleeplessness and pain . . ." is from Shorter, p. 40.

146   Patrick Brontë, "My *dear* little Anne," is quoted in Barker, p. 581.

146   Nussey, "sweetly pretty and flushed . . ." is quoted in Barker, p. 581.

146   Charlotte Brontë, "like train oil," is from Wise, vol. 2, p. 299.

146   Anne Brontë, "I hoped, that with the brave and strong . . ." is from A. Brontë, "Last Lines."

149   Anne Brontë, "Be a sister . . ." is from Wise, vol. 2, p. 335.

149   Anne Brontë, "Take courage, Charlotte . . ." is from Wise, vol. 2, p. 336.

150   Charlotte Brontë, "A year ago . . ." is from Wise, vol. 2, p. 340

nine: "OUT OF OBSCURITY I CAME"

151   Charlotte Brontë, "Sometimes . . . I have a heavy heart . . ." and "I have many comforts . . ." are from Wise, vol. 3, p. 8.

151   Charlotte Brontë, "Imagination lifted me . . ." is from Shorter 1908, vol. 2, p. 74.

152   Deputy [Charlotte Brontë], "Invention may be all right . . ." is from C. Brontë, *Shirley*, p. 141.

152   Charlotte Brontë, "He never asked himself . . ." is from C. Brontë, *Shirley*, p. 27.

154   Caroline Helstone [Charlotte Brontë], "What am I to do . . ." is from C. Brontë, *Shirley*, p. 179.

154   Charlotte Brontë, "Look at your poor girls . . ." and "You would wish to be proud . . ." are from C. Brontë, *Shirley*, p. 403.

154   Charlotte Brontë, "possessed a charm . . ." is from C. Brontë, *Shirley*, p. 205.

155   Charlotte Brontë, "I let Anne go to God . . ." is quoted in Gordon, pp. 197–98.

156   Robert Moore [Charlotte Brontë], "Am I to die without you . . ." is from C. Brontë, *Shirley*, p. 641.

156   Shirley Keeldar [Charlotte Brontë], "Die without me . . ." is from C. Brontë, *Shirley*, p. 641.

156   "enlists the purer sympathies . . ." is quoted in Alexander and Smith, p. 468.

157   Lewes, "The grand function of woman . . ." is from Allott, p. 161.

157 Charlotte Brontë, "I wish all reviewers believed . . ." and "You will — I know . . ." are from Wise, vol. 3, p. 31.

158 Charlotte Brontë, "a peculiar face . . ." is from Wise, vol. 3, p. 54.

158 Thackeray, "trembling little frame . . ." is quoted in Barker, p. 619.

158 Thackeray, "warning fragrance," is quoted in Gordon, p. 199.

159 Lucy Martineau, "I lighted plenty of candles . . ." is quoted in Barker, p. 620.

160, 161 Harriet Martineau, "I thought her the smallest creature . . ." and "cast up at me . . ." are from Martineau, p. 326.

161 Lucy Martineau, "She was so pleasant . . ." is quoted in Barker, p. 621.

161 Harriet Martineau, "red all over . . ." is quoted in Barker, p. 620.

161 "believed there were books . . ." is quoted in Brookfield and Brookfield, p. 305.

161 Ritchie, "did not look pleasant . . ." is from Ritchie, p. 270.

162 Charlotte Brontë, "He is a real grand old man," is from Wise, vol. 3, p. 117.

162 Lewes, "naughty books," is quoted in Barker, p. 641.

162 Smith, "with mingled admiration and alarm . . ." is quoted in Barker, p. 641.

162 Charlotte Brontë, "so wonderfully like Emily," is quoted in Barker, p. 641.

162 Charlotte Brontë, "Oh, Mr. Richmond . . ." is quoted in Gordon, p. 219.

163 Charlotte Brontë, "as happy almost as any I ever spent" is from Wise, vol. 3, p. 125.

164 Gaskell, "She and I quarreled . . ." is quoted in Uglow, p. 248.

164 Charlotte Brontë, "little book of rhymes" is quoted in Uglow, p. 249.

164   Charlotte Brontë, "a *cosy* winter visit" is quoted in Barker, p. 663.

164   Charlotte Brontë, "Ere long a real modesty . . ." is from Wise, vol. 3, p. 199.

165   Arnold, "past thirty and plain . . ." is from Russell, p. 15.

165   Arnold, "Ah, love, let us be true . . ." is from "Dover Beach" in Abrams, pp. 2183–84.

165   Charlotte Brontë, "The strangest thing is . . ." is from Shorter 1908, vol. 2, p. 197.

166   Charlotte Brontë, "My dear Miss Wooler . . ." is from Wise, vol. 4, p. 39.

167   Charlotte Brontë, "For strangers they were nothing . . ." is from C. Brontë, "Biographical Notice of Ellis and Acton Bell," p. 12.

ten: "I Should Fancy I Heard the Steps of the Dead"
168   Nussey, "undercurrent" and "fixed intentions" are quoted in Wise, vol. 3, p. 202.

169   Charlotte Brontë, "very happy" is from Wise, vol. 3, p. 241.

169   Charlotte Brontë, "a wonderful sight . . ." is from Wise, vol. 3, p. 251.

170   "every possible invention . . ." is from Tallis, p. 207.

171   Charlotte Brontë, "It seems as if magic . . ." is from Wise, vol. 3, p. 243.

171   Thackeray, "There's a fire and fury . . ." is quoted in Gordon, p. 237.

172, 173 Charlotte Brontë, "Like lightning it flashed . . . ," "He made me for the first time . . . ," and "Papa worked himself into a state . . ." are from Wise, vol. 4, p. 29.

173   Charlotte Brontë, "has about her an external coldness . . ." is quoted in Gordon, p. 257.

174 Lucy Snowe [Charlotte Brontë], "inadventurous, unstirred . . ." is from C. Brontë, *Villette,* p. 71.

174 Lucy Snowe [Charlotte Brontë], "she had no heart . . ." is from C. Brontë, *Villette,* p. 69.

175 Lucy Snowe [Charlotte Brontë], "My nervous system could hardly support . . ." is from C. Brontë, *Villette,* p. 151.

175 Lucy Snowe [Charlotte Brontë], "I had been left a legacy . . ." is from C. Brontë, *Villette,* p. 479.

176 Lucy Snowe [Charlotte Brontë], "It did not cease . . ." is from C. Brontë, *Villette,* p. 480.

176 "clear, forcible . . ." is from Allott, p. 203.

176 "charm of freshness" and "This book would have made her famous . . ." are from Allott, p. 178.

176 Evans, "still more wonderful book . . ." is quoted in Gordon, p. 255.

176 "very slight" is from Allott, p. 175.

176 "cynical and bitter spirit" is from Allott, p. 193.

176 Harriet Martineau, "almost intolerably painful" is from Gates, p. 253.

176 Harriet Martineau, "an atmosphere of pain" is from Gates, pp. 253–54.

176 Harriet Martineau, "all the female characters . . ." and "There are substantial . . ." are from Gates, p. 254.

177 Harriet Martineau, "We do not wonder . . ." is from Gates, p. 255.

177 Charlotte Brontë, "I know what *love* is . . ." is from Wise, vol. 4, p. 42.

177 Charlotte Brontë, "The differences of feeling . . ." is from Wise, vol. 4, p. 55.

177 Charlotte Brontë, "in a paroxysm . . ." and "Poor fellow . . ." are quoted in Barker, p. 730.

178 Charlotte Brontë, "the backwoods of America . . ." is from Wise, vol. 4, p. 70.

178 Gaskell, "half-blown back . . ." is from Chapple and Pollard, p. 242.

179 Gaskell, "beautiful in certain lights . . ." is from Chapple and Pollard, p. 243.

179 Gaskell, "sadly afraid of him . . ." is from Chapple and Pollard, p. 245.

179 Gaskell, "I am sure I should fancy . . ." is from Chapple and Pollard, p. 247.

180 Charlotte Brontë, "Father, I am not a young girl . . ." is quoted in Chapple and Pollard, p. 289.

180 Aykroyd, "Do you wish to kill your daughter?" is quoted in Chapple and Pollard, p. 289.

180 Taylor, "You talk wonderful nonsense . . ." is from Stevens, p. 120.

180 Charlotte Brontë, "I trust to love my husband . . ." is from Shorter 1896, p. 486.

182 "one of the best gentlemen . . ." and "what seems to me . . ." are quoted in Gordon, p. 306.

182 Charlotte Brontë, "Each time I see Mr. Nicholls . . ." is quoted in Barker, p. 761.

183 Charlotte Brontë, "Men don't seem to understand . . ." is from Wise, vol. 4, p. 155.

184 Charlotte Brontë, "Oh! I am not going to die . . ." is quoted in Green, p. 289.

184 Charlotte Brontë, "No kinder, better husband . . ." is quoted in Shorter 1908, vol. 2, p. 388.

afterword: "Alas!"

185   Arnold, "Early she goes . . ." is from "Haworth Churchyard" in Arnold, p. 279.

185   Martineau, "Her heroines love . . ." is from Allott, p. 302.

186   Martineau, "the coarseness . . ." is from Allott, p. 303.

186   Martineau, "vanishing from our view," is from Allott, p. 305.

186   Patrick Brontë, "I can see no better plan . . ." is quoted in Green, p. 297.

188   Patrick Brontë, "Dear Daughter Charlotte . . ." is quoted in Green, p. 293.

188   Patrick Brontë, "My grief is so deep . . ." is quoted in Barker, p. 783.

189   Auerbach, "Jane's inner world" is from Bloom, p. 57.

190   Rich, "Charlotte Brontë's feminist manifesto" is from Bloom, p. 61.

190   Spacks, "Give him a black leather jacket . . ." is from Spacks, p. 175.

190   Arnold, "Strew with roses . . ." is from "Haworth Churchyard" in Arnold, p. 279.

Selected Bibliography

Abrams, M. H., ed. *The Norton Anthology of English Literature,* 3d ed. New York: W. W. Norton and Co., 1975.

Alexander, Christine. *The Brontës: Tales of Glass Town, Angria, and Gondal.* Oxford: Oxford University Press, 2010.

———. *The Early Writings of Charlotte Brontë.* Oxford, U.K.: Basil Blackwell, 1983.

Alexander, Christine, and Margaret Smith. *The Oxford Companion to the Brontës.* Oxford, U.K.: Oxford University Press, 2003.

Allott, Miriam, ed. *The Brontës: The Critical Heritage.* London: Routledge and Kegan Paul, 1974.

Arnold, Matthew, *The Poems of Matthew Arnold, 1840–1867.* London: Henry Frowde, 1909.

Barker, Juliet. *The Brontës.* New York: St. Martin's Griffin, 1996.

Bell, Currer, Ellis Bell, and Acton Bell. *Poems.* London: Smith Elder, 1846.

Beer, Frances, ed. *The Juvenilia of Jane Austen and Charlotte Brontë.* Harmondsworth, Middlesex, U.K.: Penguin Books, 1986.

Bloom, Harold, ed. *The Brontës.* Broomall, Pa.: Chelsea House, 2000.

Brontë, Anne. *Agnes Grey.* Ware, Hertfordshire, U.K.: Wordsworth Editions, 1994.

———. "Last Lines." *The Poetry Foundation.* www.poetryfoundation.org/poem/175566. Downloaded on June 30, 2011.

———. *The Tenant of Wildfell Hall.* Ware, Hertfordshire, U.K.: Wordsworth Editions, 1994.

Brontë, Charlotte. "Biographical Notice of Ellis and Acton Bell," in *Wuthering Heights,* by Emily Brontë. New York: Dodd, Mead and Co., 1924.

———. *Jane Eyre.* London: Penguin Books, 1996.

———. *The Professor, Emma and Poems.* Boston: Estes and Lauriat, 1891.

———. *Shirley.* London: Penguin Books, 1994.

———. *Villette.* New York: Harper Colophon, 1972.

Brontë, Emily. *The Complete Poems of Emily Jane Brontë.* New York: Columbia University Press, 1995.

———. *Gondal Poems.* Oxford, U.K.: Shakespeare Head Press, 1989.

———. *Wuthering Heights.* Boston: Houghton Mifflin Co., 1956.

Brookfield, Charles, and Frances Brookfield. *Mrs. Brookfield and Her Circle.* Vol. 2. New York: Charles Scribner's Sons, 1905.

Chaplin, Sue. *Law, Sensibility and the Sublime in Eighteenth-Century Women's Fiction.* Aldershot, Hampshire, U.K.: Ashgate, 2004.

Chapple, J. A. V., and Arthur Pollard, eds. *The Letters of Mrs. Gaskell.* Manchester, U.K.: Manchester University Library, 1966.

Chitham, Edward. *The Poems of Anne Brontë: A New Text and Commentary.* Totowa, N.J.: Rowman and Littlefield, 1979.

"Christmas Dreams." *Blackwood's Edinburgh Magazine,* January 1828, pp. 1–6.

Collins, Robert G., ed. *The Hand of the Arch-Sinner: Two Angrian Chronicles of Branwell Brontë.* Oxford, U.K.: Clarendon Press, 1993.

Dormandy, Thomas. *The White Death: A History of Tuberculosis.* New York: Washington Square Press, 2000.

Ellis, Sarah Stickney. *The Women of England.* New York: D. Appleton and Co., 1839.

"An Evening's Gossip on New Novels." *Dublin University Magazine,* May 1848, pp. 608–25.

Gaskell, E. C. *The Life of Charlotte Brontë.* Edinburgh: John Grant, 1905.

Gates, Barbara Timm. *Critical Essays on Charlotte Brontë.* Boston: G. K. Hall and Co., 1990.

Gordon, Lyndall. *Charlotte Brontë: A Passionate Life.* New York: W. W. Norton and Co., 1995.

Green, Dudley. *Patrick Brontë: Father of Genius.* Stroud, Gloucestershire, U.K.: Nonsuch, 2008.

Grundy, Francis H. *Pictures of the Past: Memories of Men I Have Met and Places I Have Seen.* London: Griffith and Farrar, 1879.

Harrison, Ada M., and Derek Stanford. *Anne Brontë: Her Life and Work.* Hamden, Conn.: Archon Books, 1970.

Hoar, Nancy Cowley. "'And My Ending Is Despair': *Villette* — Charlotte Brontë's Valediction." *Brontë Society Transactions,* 1973, pp. 185–235.

Howe, Bea. *A Galaxy of Governesses.* London: Derek Verschoyle, 1954.

"The Last New Novel." *The Mirror.* December 1847, pp. 376–80.

Lewes, George Henry. "Recent Novels: French and English." *Fraser's Magazine for Town and Country,* December 1847, pp. 686–95.

Leyland, Francis A. *The Brontë Family, with Special Reference to Patrick Branwell Brontë.* Vol. 2. London: Hurst and Blackett, 1886.

Lock, John, and W. T. Dixon. *A Man of Sorrow: The Life, Letters and Times of the Rev. Patrick Brontë, 1777–1861.* London: Ian Hodgkins and Co., 1979.

Lonoff, Sue, ed. and trans. *The Belgian Essays.* New Haven, Conn.: Yale University Press, 1996.

Martineau, Harriet. *Harriet Martineau's Autobiography.* London: Virago Press, 1983.

Neufeldt, Victor A., ed. *The Poems of Patrick Branwell Brontë.* New York: Garland Publishing, 1990.

"Noteworthy Novels." *North British Review,* August 1849, pp. 475–93.

Orel, Harold, ed. *The Brontës: Interviews and Recollections.* Iowa City: University of Iowa Press, 1997.

"Patrick Brontë Chronology." *Haworth Village.* www.haworth-village. org.uk. Downloaded on January 16, 2011.

Rees, Joan. *Profligate Son: Branwell Brontë and His Sisters.* London: Robert Hale, 1986.

Ritchie, Hester, ed. *Letters of Anne Thackeray Ritchie.* London: John Murray, 1924.

Russell, George W. E., ed. *Letters of Matthew Arnold, 1848–1888.* Vol. 1. New York: Macmillan and Co., 1895.

Scruton, William. *Thornton and the Brontës.* Bradford, U.K.: John Dale and Co., 1898.

Shorter, Clement. *The Brontës: Life and Letters.* London: Hodder and Stoughton, 1908.

———. *Charlotte Brontë and Her Circle.* London: Hodder and Stoughton, 1896.

Sinclair, May. *The Three Brontës.* Boston: Houghton Mifflin, 1913.

Smith, Elizabeth, ed. *George Smith: A Memoir, with Some Pages of Autobiography.* London: Privately printed, 1902.

Smithers, Henry. *Liverpool: Its Commerce, Statistics, and Institutions.* Liverpool, England: Thomas Kaye, 1825.

Spacks, Patricia Meyer. *The Female Imagination.* New York: Alfred A. Knopf, 1975.

Stevens, Joan, ed. *Mary Taylor: Friend of Charlotte Brontë.* Dunedin, New Zealand: Auckland University Press, 1972.

Tallis, John. *Tallis' History and Description of the Crystal Palace, and the Exhibition of the World's Industry in 1851.* Vol. 1. London: John Tallis and Co., 1852.

Thackeray, William Makepeace. *Vanity Fair.* Leipzig, Germany: Bernhard Tauchnitz, 1848.

Turner, J. Horsfall. *Brontëana: The Rev. Patrick Brontë, A.B., His Collected Works and Life.* Folcroft, Pa.: Folcroft Library Editions, 1974.

Uglow, Jenny. *Elizabeth Gaskell: A Habit of Stories.* London: Faber and Faber, 1993.

Vivian. "A Gentle Hint to Writing-Women." *Leader,* May 18, 1850, p. 189.

Ward, John. *Information Relative to New-Zealand.* 1840. Christchurch, New Zealand: Capper Press, 1975.

Whitehead, Barbara. *Charlotte Brontë and Her "Dearest Nell": The Story of a Friendship.* West Yorkshire, U.K.: Smith Settle, 1993.

Willy, Margaret. "Emily Brontë: Poet and Mystic." *English,* autumn 1946, pp. 117–22.

Wilson, William Carus. "On Patience and Forbearance in a Sunday-School Teacher." *The Teacher's Visitor,* January 1847, pp. 21–22.

Winnifrith, Tom, ed. *The Poems of Charlotte Brontë.* Oxford, U.K.: Shakespeare Head Press, 1984.

Wise, Thomas J., ed. *The Brontës: Their Lives, Friendships and Correspondence.* 4 vols. Philadelphia: Porcupine Press, 1980.

The Works of Charlotte, Emily and Anne Brontë. Vol. 8: *Poems of Currer, Ellis and Acton Bell with Cottage Poems by Patrick Brontë.* London: J. M. Dent and Co., 1893.

"Wuthering Heights." *Leader,* December 28, 1850, p. 953.

The Works of
Charlotte, Emily, and Anne
Brontë

Writing as Currer, Ellis, and Acton Bell, the Brontë sisters collaborated on a collection of poetry. As individuals they completed seven novels that were intended for publication. These classic works have appeared in numerous editions, but the following were the first:

Poems, by Currer, Ellis, and Acton Bell. London: Aylott and Jones, 1846.

Jane Eyre, by Currer Bell. London: Smith, Elder and Company, 1847.

Wuthering Heights, by Ellis Bell. London: T. C. Newby, 1847.

Agnes Grey, by Acton Bell. London: T. C. Newby, 1847.

The Tenant of Wildfell Hall, by Acton Bell. London: T. C. Newby, 1848.

Shirley, by Currer Bell. London: Smith, Elder and Company, 1849.

Villette, by Currer Bell. London: Smith, Elder and Company, 1853.

The Professor, by Currer Bell. London: Smith, Elder and Company, 1857.

The Brontës wrote a great many letters, although not all of them have survived. A complete collection has yet to be published, but this one is large and comprehensive:

The Brontës: Their Lives, Friendships, and Correspondence (4 vols.), edited by Thomas J. Wise. Philadelphia: Porcupine Press, 1980.

Readers interested in the Brontës' childhood writings can refer to:

Tales of Glass Town, Angria, and Gondal, edited by Christine Alexander. Oxford, U.K.: Oxford University Press, 2010.

Picture Credits

Index

Page numbers in *italic* type refer to illustrations and their captions.

Brontë, Branwell *(cont.)*
   self-image, 14
   self-portrait, *41*
   as tutor, 53–55, 73, *74,*
     83–84
Brontë, Charlotte. See also
   Jane Eyre
   Angria and Gondal
     fantasies, 17–18, *19,*
     31–32
   with Anne at time of
     death, *147,* 147–49
   aspiration to become
     writer, 14, 34
   on Austen's novels, 97
   biography of, 187–88
   at Clergy Daughters'
     School, 6–9, 11, *11*
   depression, 22, 32, 78, 172
   diary paper, 15
   drawing and painting,
     30, *30, 42, 56,* 57
   on Emily's death, 144,
     155
   friendships at school,
     21–22, 23–24, 68, 76
   Gaskell, Elizabeth,
     friendship with, 163–
     64, *178,* 178–79, 186–
     87

Brontë, Charlotte *(cont.)*
   as governess, 48–51,
     60–61
   hero, Duke of
     Wellington, 5, 16,
     27, 161–62
   home education, 11–12
   illness and death, 183–
     86
   independence, 23, 51,
     75
   on Maria's death, 10
   marriage, *181,* 181–83
   marriage proposals,
     43–44, 51, 172–73,
     180–81
Martineau, Harriet,
   friendship with, 159–
   61, *160,* 165, 176–
   77, 185–86
   move to Haworth
     parsonage, 2–3
   at Pensionnat Heger
     school, 61–65, *63,*
     66–68, 78–80
   physical appearance and
     poor eyesight, 14, 22,
     77, 134–35
   plan to open own
     school, 61, 82–83, *84*